JAMAICA'S REGGAE BOYS
WORLD CUP 1998

Starters at the beginning of the final round
Back: *Warren Barrett (Capt), Theodore Whitmore, Durrent Brown, Peter Cargill, Ian Goodison, Walter Boyd, trainer Professor Montesso*
Front: *Dean Sewell, Linval Dixon, Gregory Messam, Andy Williams, Steve Malcolm.*

JAMAICA'S REGGAE BOYS
WORLD CUP 1998

Earl Bailey and Nazma Muller

Ian Randle Publishers *and* Creative Communications Inc.

© Earl Bailey and Nazma Muller

First published 1998 by
Ian Randle Publishers Limited
206 Old Hope Road, Box 686
Kingston 6, Jamaica

and

Creative Communications Inc.
P.O. Box 105
Kingston 10, Jamaica

All rights reserved—no part of this publication may be reproduced, stored in a retrieval system, or transmitted in any form or by any means electronic, photocopying, recording or otherwise without the prior permission of the publishers

ISBN 976 8123 72 9 Paperback

A catalogue record for this book is available from the National Library of Jamaica

Book design by Prodesign Ltd., Red Gal Ring, Kingston 8, Jamaica

ACKNOWLEDGMENTS

The publishers acknowledge with gratitude the assistance given by *The Jamaica Observer* and *The Daily Gleaner* newspapers in sourcing photographs and to their cartoonists, Clovis and Las May. Special thanks go to Lindy Delapenha and to Colonel Ken Barnes and his wife Jean for providing information and photographs; also to Brian Rosen for his photograph of the National Stadium, as well as to Don Streete, a one of a kind Reggae Boys fan, for giving access to his collection of match memorabilia. We thank the National Library of Jamaica for giving us access to their football clippings and Joan Andrea Hutchinson and Papa San for the use of their tributes to the Reggae Boys.

CONTENTS

Introduction: Stepping into history *6*

The Story of Jamaican Football *8*
       Launching the National Program and Flashback to the early Years

Step One: The semi-final round 1996 . . . . . *27*

Step Two: The final round 1997 . . . . . *37*

       USA – March 2, Kingston *38*

       Mexico – April 13, Mexico City *44*

       Canada – April 27, Vancouver *52*

       Costa Rica – May 11, San Jose *58*

       El Salvador – May 18, Kingston *62*

       Canada – September 7, Kingston *68*

       Costa Rica – September 14, Kingston *74*

       USA – October 3, Washington D.C. *82*

       El Salvador – November 9, San Salvador *92*

       Mexico – November 16, Kingston *96*

Epilogue *104*

INTRODUCTION—STEPPING

It is clear that the Mexicans, assured of their place in France, are more interested in avoiding defeat than winning. They are reluctant to engage in the warfare which would undoubtedly occur if they attempt to storm the Jamaican defence. When captain Luis Garcia finally takes a shot at goal in the 20th minute, it is with some reluctance and not much conviction.

Though there is nothing to cheer about on the field, the home fans are exulting in every goalless moment the Mexicans let pass.

The loudspeaker crackles, but is barely heard above the happy stadium noise. Then what a hullabaloo breaks out! The cheers build up across the stadium as the word is passed along. The announcer comes on again. Thousands of miles away in Boston, the US has scored its first goal against El Salvador!

The Eiffel Tower is on the horizon.

The Reggae Boys appear not to have heard, focused as they are on keeping the Mexicans away from their goalpost. Then, a hush comes over the crowd. Rumours of an El Salvadorean equaliser come next. Minutes later, the screams are louder: USA has scored again. The celebrations begin again. **"France, we comin!"**

By now, everyone has stopped watching the match and is prancing around to the joyous sounds of dancehall. For a moment, the thought that they might actually run on to the field before the final whistle blows and stop the match paralyses the paranoid. After all the Reggae Boys have gone through, to be disqualified would be a curse by the gods.

The USA scores a third goal; there is no hope for El Salvador. People stop and stare at each other: Jamaica is going to the World Cup finals . . .

At the University of the West Indies campus in St Augustine, Jamaican students were seen running with their flags—sheer joy on their faces, the wind whipping the black, gold and green as they tore across the campus.

Shouts echoed across Flatbush Avenue as the news sank in. The boomboxes started blasting all through Brooklyn as Likkle Jamaica celebrated. In Washington, in London, in Australia, in every country across the world, tears of joy and pride tumbled down Jamaican cheeks.

And across the Caribbean, Trinidadians, Barbadians, St Lucians, Dominicans, Cubans, Martiniquans, Haitians, they all cheered for the men with undeniable courage and character whose determination spoke for them all.

The Cubans remembered 1938 wistfully, when their team had made it to the World Cup finals; in Haiti, 1974 seemed such a long time ago. Twenty-four years

INTO HISTORY

later, another Caribbean country, this time an English-speaking one, had staked its place among the giants of the sport.

Out of Africa in 1994 had come the Cameroons, challenging the first world professionals. Now, out of the Caribbean, a team from an island known mainly for its music, its beaches, a failing economy and a terrifying crime rate, had stepped onto the world stage, one of the players barely 19, to attest to the raw talent and indomitable will of the Jamaican people.

Pride seared through our hearts because you see, we all knew how far the Reggae Boys had come . . .

◀ *Dean Sewell makes a run into history*

The lead story in the Jamaica Observer *said it all on November 17, 1997*

THE STORY OF JAMAICAN

Launching the National Program

Jamaica's relatively recent football history has two stages. The second stage which began with the launching of a national program and preparations for the 1998 World Cup finals began in 1994 when there were two significant developments. In June of that year former army officer Horace Burrell was elected president of the Jamaica Football Federation (JFF) and immediately declared his intention to take Jamaica to the 1998 World Cup finals. Burrell who was then a vice-president of the Caribbean Football Union realized that Jamaican football had to go through a major transformation if the dream of rising to world class level was to become a reality. He also realized that two elements were vital in this process of building a national program – money (and lots of it) and the services of a top-class coach, preferably from Brazil – a country whose football achievements and skills Jamaicans admired and craved with an almost religious zeal.

The search for a Brazilian coach unearthed the diminutive Rene Simoes who arrived in Jamaica in October 1994 to assume the position of national technical director of football. By then Burrell had put together an impressive team comprising some of the country's top business leaders who were charged with the responsibility of raising the kind of money that was needed to support the program. In Simoes the JFF had acquired a football professional with undoubted technical skill but also a stern disciplinarian and, above all, one who shared the vision that Jamaicans possessed the latent talent and skill to take them to the highest levels of world football.

This was not Jamaica's first attempt at qualifying for the World Cup. Another Brazilian coach Jorge Penna had tried back in the mid-sixties to help Jamaica qualify for the 1966 finals in England. Penna assembled a squad comprising goalkeepers Don Clarke and Duke Fuller; defenders Frank Brown, Henry Largie and Erkle Vaz; midfielders Syd Bartlett, Jackie Bell and Neville Glanville and forwards Oscar Black, Lascelles Dunkley, Art and Asher Welsh.

The team had limited success, beating Cuba and the Netherlands Antilles in the Caribbean zone. But their shortcomings were exposed when they moved to the CONCACAF playoffs and were no match for Costa Rica to whom they lost 3-0 in San Jose and Mexico who gave them a 7-0 drubbing in Mexico City after the Jamaicans had narrowly lost 2-3 at home in the first match.

Prior to the 1966 World Cup campaign Jamaica had played very little football at the international level. Most of the games were friendlies, for which teams were hastily put together by a part-time coach. Haiti, Trinidad and Tobago and Cuba were among the countries facing Jamaica. In the absence of a local professional league or regular international matches, talented footballers joined clubs overseas

Carlton 'Puskas' Smith playing for Jamaica against the Dominican Republic in 1975

FOOTBALL

Lascelles Dunkley, left, and Art Welch

The 1948 Jamaican team that played Haiti

to develop their skills and earn a living. The first exodus of players from Jamaica took place in the mid-1960s when a number of players left to join clubs in Canada. They were to be followed later by players who went to join clubs in the USA where a professional football (soccer) league had just been established. Among the early players to join this trek to North America were Art and Asher Welsh, Syd Bartlett, Alan 'Skill' Cole, Henry Largie, Dennis Zadie, Lloyd McLean, Ruddy Pearce and Allie McNab.

In the annals of Jamaican football history two individuals stand out as being the greatest players ever produced by this country. Lindy Delapenha and John Barnes both made their marks on the other side of the Atlantic playing for English clubs and in the case of Barnes, for England including the 1986 World Cup finals in Mexico. Although neither player appeared for Jamaica on the international scene, (although Lindy Delapenha did play once for Jamaica against a Caribbean all-stars team in 1950) their exploits on behalf of their adopted teams made them true stars at the international level.

Alan 'Skill' Cole, one of the great Jamaican players

Lindy Delapenha
Britain's first Jamaican footballer

If you were in Portsmouth, England, in 1947, a short report in the local newspaper's football section might have caught your eye: "Since the days of Leslie (Plymouth) and Parris (Bradford) no coloured player has secured a regular place in a league side, but I am told, Portsmouth may include one next season. A month ago they signed on Lloyd Lindburgh (sic) Delapenha, a twenty year-old inside right from Jamaica, who is also no mean cricketer and has been booked for a trial with Hants."

Lloyd Lindbergh "Lindy" Delapenha was born in Jamaica in 1927 and attended Wolmers and Munro College before leaving for Britain where he lived for 18 years. An outstanding sportsman and athlete at high school, Lindy also represented the British Army in football, cricket, athletics and hockey.

It was while playing for the army that he was scouted and signed in April, 1948, by the English First Division Football League side, Portsmouth, having chosen the south coast club over Chelsea and Plymouth. The future prospects for the 21-year old Delapenha, playing in his debut game against Blackpool with its legendary forwards Matthews and Mortensen, were described in the newspaper headline . . . **"Jamaican makes promising start with Portsmouth"**.

Before long he was a regular member of the senior team and being touted by the U.K. press as being "potentially one of the best inside forwards in the game." During the three years he was with Portsmouth his team won the first Division Championship.

In 1950 Lindy was transferred to another First Division team, Middlesborough F.C. where he won a well-deserved reputation as a quick-thinking hard-shooting right winger who set up countless scoring opportunities for his teammates.

On one occasion he had the special pleasure of taking his new team to the top of the league—winning their twelfth consecutive game—by contributing a goal in Middlesborough's 3-1 victory over Portsmouth before 34,000 fans. The local soccer reporter wrote: "Portsmouth is his old club and, as often happens, the player was out to demonstrate the extent to which his powers had been underestimated when he was allowed to leave. Most pleasing feature of all was that the MIddlesborough man kept his head when opponents became irate and, having failed to get the ball, took the man instead. It was an afternoon Delapenha will long remember, especially since his goal ten minutes from the end extinguished Portsmouth hopes, and rounded off a great afternoon's work."

Lindy earned an enviable reputation as the club's penalty-taker. His then teammate, Brian Clough, who went on to become Nottingham Forest's controversially successful manager, when asked why he never took Middlesborough's penalties replied **". . . because Lindy never bloody misses!"**

The Story of Jamaican Football

In 1954 Lindy was on the team that, after 25 years First Division prominence, was relegated to the Second Division after its final game against Arsenal. The next day's headline read: **Delapenha's Dash Not Enough**. By this time he had played 270 League and Cup games and scored an impressive 93 goals. He subsequently played for Mansfield Town before being forced out of professional soccer with a groin injury at age 33. He returned to Jamaica in 1964 as football coach to the Appleton sugar estate.

Lindy Delapenha was the first Jamaican and probably the first black player to earn a regular place on a British First Division team. His success on the playing field was not only reflected in the weekly press headlines praising his performance but also by the disciplined and mature manner in which he conducted himself on and off the field.

A FINE ACTION PICTURE of Lindy Delapenha, who has one of the most powerful shots in League football...

Two great Delapenha goals beat Derby

12   The Reggae Boys

The rich tapestry of Lindy's football career

The Story of Jamaican Football

Johnny Barnes
The greatest footballer Jamaica has ever produced

On June 19, 1984 England beat Brazil for the first time in 28 years. Two factors made the occasion unforgettable: the first was that the 2-nil victory took place in Rio de Janeiro's awesome Maracana Stadium. The second was that Johnny Barnes, in beating five defenders to score a sensational goal, prompted the Brazilian superstar Zico to predict that **"The future of English football lies with John Barnes."** Jimmy Greaves, the former English centre forward, described Barnes' performance as "The greatest goal scored in an English shirt."

This historic moment was also to foreshadow his dramatically successful but disappointingly brief appearance in the 1986 World Cup in Mexico.

It might not have been difficult to predict that John Barnes at birth was destined to become one of the world's great sportsmen. His father, Colonel Ken Barnes, a native Trinidadian, played football for Jamaica, captained the team in the mid-sixties and went on to become its manager. His mother, Jean, herself an active sportswoman, came from a family of sport-loving men and women. Johnny's cousin, Anthony, an inside right is considered along with Sidney Bartlett and Allan "Skill" Cole to be one of Jamaica's most outstanding national representatives.

Weaned on the playing fields of Up-Park Camp, broken in at Mico All-Age School and making his senior-school debut as an 11-year old in St. George's College's Under-16 side, John Barnes lived, breathed and played football from the day his sister Gillian first tapped a ball towards his tiny feet.

Fate intervened in 1975 when Colonel Barnes was assigned to the Jamaican High Commission in London as military attaché. Ironically, Johnny's first school played rugby—he even went for an Under-16 county team trial—so he played soccer with Stowe Boys Club on weekends. Roy Sullivan, Stowe's manager, also managed Sudbury Court in the amateur Middlesex League. By age 16, Johnny with ten goals, first made his mark when Sudbury won the senior league losing only three out of 33 games.

His contribution drew the attention of former Arsenal great Bertie Mee, Watford F.C.'s general manager, who persuaded the Barnes family to allow Johnny to sign up in April, 1981. On September 5, he was substituted for 15 minutes against Oldham Athletic. His full debut came against Chelsea the following week. He was still only 17 years old. Manager Grahame Taylor, later to become England's manager, remarked after the game, **"I think I have a jewel in that boy!"**

Good fortune was once again on Johnny's side. Taylor was in the process of taking Watford from the Fourth to the First Division which he did in only five seasons. Taylor was lucky too, as rock star Elton John opened up his cheque book to his home town team.

Watford had probably England's best organized young player programme; Barnes also had teammate Luther Blissett, of Jamaican parentage, to mentor him.

Barnes uses his awesome power and skill to make another attack for Liverpool

16 The Reggae Boys

John's extraordinary ball-control skills, unreserved commitment and imaginative plays won him a call to the England Under-21 squad by the time he was 19. This was to be the first of 79 England caps for him.

He played in Watford's 1984 encounter with a powerful Everton team in the 1984 F.A. Cup and later that same summer came to the world's attention in England's spectacular victory in Rio.

His playing career for England was one of spectacular successes mixed with inexplicable off-days. When England reached the final rounds of the 1986 Mexico World Cup Chris Waddle was appearing more frequently in Barnes' familiar left-wing position. However, when Johnny came off the bench with 15 minutes left against Argentina—a game remembered for Diego Maradona's questionable 'hand of God' goal—he fed Gary Lineker with two superb good-scoring chances, one of which he converted to almost save England's day.

Johnny Barnes, the first black player to appear regularly for Liverpool, began changing the ideas of the city's white football culture by scoring one goal and setting up a second in the team's first home game. Liverpool were undefeated for its first 29 games winning the First Division League title with just two losses in 40 games.

The freedom of movement on the field that Johnny enjoyed released him and his talent from the more conventional long ball game he knew at Watford.

Over the next two seasons he was named English Player of the Year on consecutive occasions and saw his team triumph in 1989 over fierce city rivals Everton by three goals to two in the F. A. Cup. His goal-scoring ability was shown at its best in the 1989/90 season when he scored 28—two more than Ian Rush, his perennially prolific partner.

Liverpool's fortunes were not to rise to such heights again in the early nineties and although John Barnes had expressed an inclination to play in Italy where his brand of skill and flair were prized, he remained with the northern team and ultimately became its captain.

In 1998 he left for Newcastle United, rejoined his former Liverpool manager Kenny Dalglish, where he scored freely until injury sidelined him. His comprehensive knowledge and understanding of the game of football has earned him a place on Thames Television's 1998 World Cup broadcast team.

▲ *John Barnes captured in his All-Stars strip when he played in Jamaica in 1986 against a Peruvian team*

Striking for Liverpool

◀ *Barnes the ball–et dancer! Spectacular mid-air ball control was one of Barnes' distinctive skills*

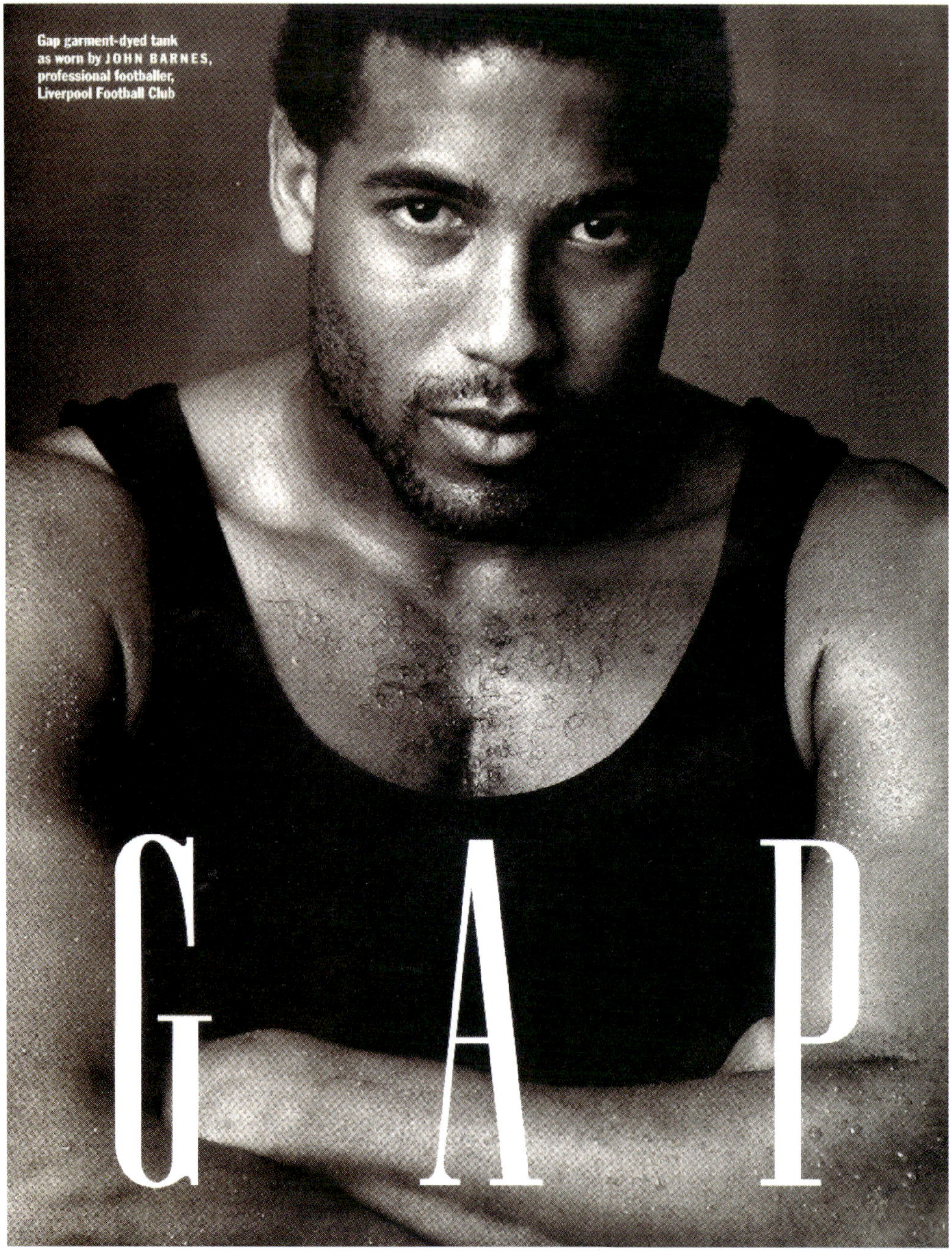
Gap garment-dyed tank
as worn by JOHN BARNES,
professional footballer,
Liverpool Football Club
GAP

The Guardian
Tide swells against Krenz

Mirror

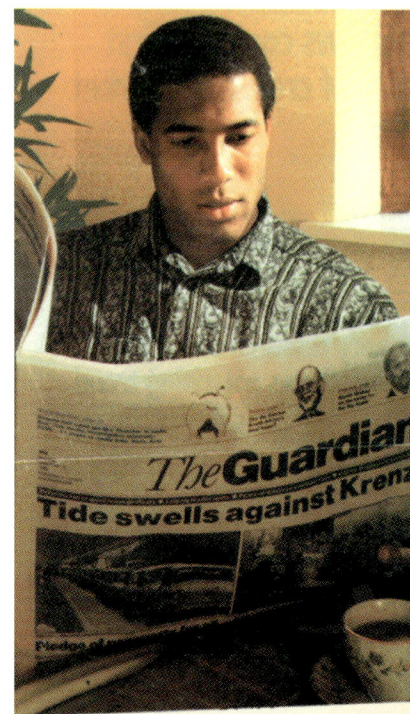

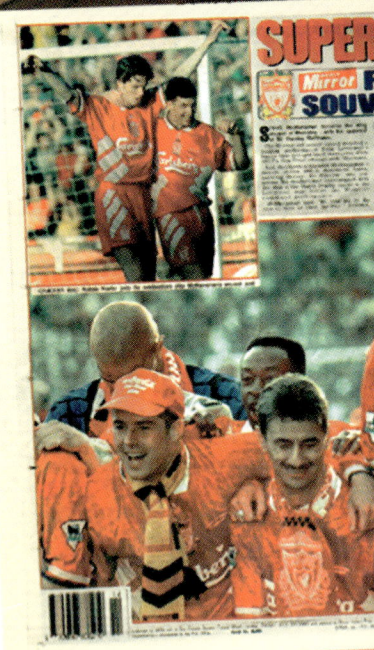

John Barnes, an advertisers dream: Super Model for GAP casual wear . . . and above right, no, he isn't endorsing The Guardian*, but rather the coffee he is drinking*

Johnny was one of the best things that happened for the U.K. Crown Paint brand (Liverpool's sponsor) for a decade!

▲ *Powering through his opponents for Liverpool*

◄ *The Daily Mirror hails Liverpool's 2-1 victor, over Bolton Wonderers in the 1995 Coca-Cola Cup Final at Wembley*

His style and artistry ensured that he wasn't just another player on the field . . . he was the focal point

The long and winding road . . .

Football in Jamaica, you see, is not the institution it is in Brazil, or a business, like in Europe where there are major leagues and football is actually a career option. Football in Jamaica is just a game. Or it used to be.

Up to the 1950s, three decades after the national team first played its first international match against Haiti in 1925 (the Haitians were beaten three times: 2-1, 3-0 and 1-0), Jamaica had played only against the French colony, other British colonies in the region, club teams and teams from visiting ships.

The first team had been started by Rev GC Hardwicke at York Castle School in St Ann in 1893. That same year several members, upon leaving school, formed the first Kingston team. By 1898 the Jamaica Association of Football had a league competition going, a challenge shield the main attraction. In 1910, the Jamaica Football Association was formed. Different competitions were started in the first few decades of the 20th century, with individuals offering cups and shield—Sir Sydney Olivier donated the Olivier Sield in 1910 and Governor Sir William Manning donated the still coveted Cup in 1914, both trophies to be played for by school boys.

The cricket clubs ruled the game, the Kingston Cricket Club being the first to introduce the sport. Most games were played in the Corporate Area—Kingston and St Andrew—with only one other parish, St James, having an organised team. Clubs like Railway, Army Local and Army Foreign (made up of English soldiers) were the major competitors.

The first big matches to draw interest took place in 1950 between a Caribbean All Stars team of players from Suriname, Trinidad, Cuba and Haiti and a Jamaican side with professionals like Gillie Heron and Lindy Delapenha. Club

A star forward of the 1920's, Lambert Lewis

The first Jamaican international team . . . a faded memory

football eventually gained support, and Arthur McKenzie, Claude McMorris, Noel Hall, Henry Miller, Lester Alcock, Bobby Williams and Digger Largie made their names during the era before independence.

It was only after 1962, when Jamaica became eligible for regional and international football competitions as a full member of FIFA (Federation Internationale de Football Association), including the World Cup, that matches against Mexico, Venezuela, Puerto Rico, Honduras, Guatemala, Panama and Costa Rica would be played.

By then each parish was to have its own association, and a national football team was put on the agenda. Preparations began for the British Commonwealth Games in 1966. It was at this time that Jorge Penna was hired as coach and members of the national team received training gear. Before that, each man had to provide his own boots and shorts, and after every international match, return his uniform to an official waiting at the door of the changing room. A salary was not even considered; it was all to be done for love of the game. One player, Pinkie Smith, used to row his boat from Port Royal, dock at King Street, jog to Sabina Park, play, then return home the same way.

Playing against Guyana in 1973

By the 1970s, the game had switched from being club-based to community-based; and the sport exploded as teams sprang up in every major town in most parishes. But the rise in popularity did not escape the attention of what was the beginning of Jamaica's "tribal politics" history. Violence became a part of football games, and the sport lost many players turned off by its politicisation.

There was no stopping the interest in the game though, and in 1972 when Jamaica beat Mexico 1-0 in an Olympic qualifying match at the National Stadium, the sweet taste of victory over the Central American champions ensured the country's continued obsession with the game.

By the 1980s cricket was hard-pressed to maintain its status as the national sport. Premier, major and community leagues were being played throughout the week, and even more so on Saturday and Sunday evenings. In the ghettos of Tivoli Gardens and Arnett Gardens, self-esteem would be found on the football field as these two teams led the club rankings, along with Boys Town, Cavalier, Santos, Reno, Harbour View and Nascimento.

But a national team of any repute was still a hazy mirage on the horizon. Wins were never guaranteed and losses occurred all too unexpectedly, and frequently. By 1991, the one international title Jamaica had to its name was the Shell Caribbean Cup. Third place in the CONCACAF Gold Cup came in 1993 under coach Carl Brown, a former national player.

One year later, the Jamaica Football Federation got a new president, a new technical director, a new road (the Road to France), and everyone knew football was never going to be just a game again in Jamaica.

Rene Simoes
The director of dreams

"If Jah is standing by my side, why should I be afraid?" sang Tony Rebel. Rene Simoes would probably agree; perhaps changing it to say, If Christ is on the Reggae Boys' side, they should not be afraid.

The technical director of the national team who wears his "Jesus Saves" T-shirt to every match has become something akin to a messiah, as well as a professor of the game.

The man who coached the Brazilian Under-20 national team to victory in 1988 in the South American Youth Championship in Argentina has, one decade later, shocked the world and written a new chapter in Jamaican history by taking the national team to the World Cup finals in France.

It would have been strange for a Brazilian to dream of taking a Jamaican team to the World Cup; the Brazilian team maybe, but certainly not the Jamaicans. And it would have been a nightmare in which this little Caribbean island had actually beaten the World Cup champions. Simoes admits that getting the Reggae Boys French visas was not what he thought of as he counted sheep at nights. Horace Burrell was doing that. As Simoes the storyteller writes in his account of his first encounter with the president of the football federation in the JFF's *The Road to France* publication (1997): "There was once an army captain who knew how to make bread and liked football. He was elected president of the football federation and went to sleep dreaming of a Brazilian coach to direct his national team."

At the time of Capt. Burrell's arrival in Rio in 1994 in search of his Brazilian coach, Simoes was with a third division football club, Mesquita. He had recently returned from Qatar where he had taken the Doha-Qatar club team from one victory to another in a five-year period.

"I had no intentions of coming to Jamaica," Simoes wrote in *The Road to France*. "I had been here once and knew that the conditions were very difficult."

But "it's love at first sight, there's no way out," Brazilian officials told him. Everyone, the minister of education, the minister of external relations, the chief ambassador for Caribbean matters, was asking him to accept Burrell's offer.

The "short man with a moustache", as he describes himself, has a knack for storytelling that is well-known and documented (in a series of columns published by the *Observer*); and his quotes are always endearingly frank.

One of 12 children born to working class parents in Cavalcante, Rio de Janeiro, close to ghetto areas not unlike Trench Town, the Brazilian believes God gave him a talent, and that he is to facilitate others. Almost half a century ago, in another dream his mother saw a little boy sitting beside a football with a whistle around his neck. That was the night before he was born.

—Norman Grindley

Rene Simoes, technical director of the national football team, displays his talents at the Life of Jamaica (LoJ) Centre, New Kingston where LoJ presented a computer and printer to the Bustamante Hospital for Children. Each member of the national team was required to kick a football into a small six-a-side goal. Each goal was valued at $3,000 and the score stopped at the computer cost.

Simoes in a rare quiet moment. He never sits on the bench during a game, studyng the other team intently before shouting orders to his men

The same night he was finally convinced by Burrell to come to Jamaica, Simoes received a more lucrative offer from a Japanese team. But the Brazilian had given his word. And he kept it.

"Today I am happy the word won," he writes.

So is Jamaica, Simoes, so is Jamaica.

Simoes' track record

Simoes' success as a coach and manager goes back almost two decades before the climax of Jamaica's qualification for the World Cup. As early as 1976 he began his winning streak with Somley College in Rio de Janeiro at the University Olympic Day Tournament. The following two years it was the Officers School Merchant Marine of Brazil team in the Merc-Nav Games then Somley again in the state of Rio de Janeiro University Tournament.

The 80s saw him moving on to international championships. In 1988 he led the Brazilian Under-20 national team to first place in the South American Youth Championship in Argentina and the Friendship Tournament in Spain; and the Under-18 national team in their division of the South American Youth Championship in Ecuador.

The following year he led the national team to third place in the World Cup Under-20; and the Esporte Club Bahia to wins in the second and third legs of the Bahia State Championship. Within a year he was doing the same half-way across the world in Qatar where he showed Rayan Sports Club how to take top honours in the National Championship of Qatar (for two years straight), and the Independence Cup of Qatar ('90-'91) as well as the Emir Cup ('92-'93). In 1993, he moved to another club, Arabi Sports Club, who promptly took the National Championship and runner-up place in the Emir Cup.

Simoes and Alan 'Skill' Cole discuss tactics with a young fan

Horace Burrell
Four years was all he needed

Captain Horace Burrell is, on top of everything else, a just man. While kudos have been pouring in for his work as president of the Jamaica Football Federation in spearheading the World Cup campaign, Burrell admits that it wasn't his idea.

"The entire concept of this came from FIFA vice-president and CONCACAF president, Jack Warner," he told BWIA *Caribbean Beat* in its December 1997 issue. "The initiative came in Mr Warner's hotel room in Orlando, Florida, during the 1994 World Cup in the United States. I had taken over the presidency of the Jamaican Football Federation and sought his advice on the direction to take to raise the level of our football. He gave me the blueprint." Warner's prescription included a top foreign coach and a federation to deal with the business aspect.

Simple enough, but requiring meticulous planning, and a lot of hard work. Football in Jamaica had been struggling for years—the public was indifferent to the sport, and in 1994, the economy was clearly not encouraging corporate sponsors to put their money in the field. When the former army captain announced his proposal to get Jamaica to France, the cynics laughed aloud. Firstly, the players were unpaid for playing football; a few were employed, many unemployed; some partially supported by their clubs, others totally unsupported. Football was not a career option; and it was reflected when the team played paid professionals.

Burrell came up with an Adopt-A-Player programme in which the private sector would sponsor a team member in return for promotion and advertising of their product. He approached Prime Minister P. J. Patterson who endorsed the campaign. Burrell now had to find himself a Brazilian coach. He approached the Brazilian ambassador who contacted the president-director of the Brazilian Football Academy. The captain was on his way to Rio. There he convinced the Brazilian government to pay for his expenses in their country.

On meeting Rene Simoes, Burrell decided he was going to be Jamaica's coach. Simoes refused. Burrell then convinced Brazilian government officials that Simoes was the man. In turn they encouraged Simoes to accept the offer.

The JFF president then got the Brazilian government to pay for the first three months of Simoes' salary and expenses by creating a project of technical co-operation for the Caribbean for which Simoes would be responsible.

The professor didn't stand a chance against the army captain's negotiating skills. By October 1994, Simoes was in Jamaica, ready to begin a four-year programme that would take Jamaica, which had never won more than one Shell Cup (in 1991) and third place in the Gold Cup (1993) to the World Cup finals.

Knocking heads ... Burrell in deep conversation with Leader of the Opposition Edward Seaga, while Prime Minister P. J. Patterson (left) *watches as the team warms up before a game*

By 1995, Jamaica had earned FIFA's award to the most improved team as they moved from 98 to 56 in world ranking. In 1996 the climb continued from 56 to 32, missing the award by just one point this time.

Meanwhile Burrell had set to work on the private sector, and by 1997 a single JFF publication—*Jamaica, The Road to France*—had 86 sponsors. The Federation moved from its tiny office on Merrick Avenue to four floors of a New Kingston building. The Reggae Boys' schedule became hectic, with training camps in different countries and friendly internationals being played all over the world.

Capt. Horace Burrell had decided he was going to make a professional team out of them, and he did.

Carl Brown – Team Coach

As a schoolboy Carl Brown played for Trench Town Comprehensive High which won the coveted Manning Cup in 1969. He went on to play for the well-known Boys Town. His ability and style was difficult to miss, and inevitably he was recruited for the national team of which he became captain.

After representing the country at home and abroad for a few years, Brown retired, but not from the field returning to Boys Town to coach. This he did successfully, leading them to Major League and Premier League titles.

Meanwhile, one coach after another was failing to take the national team to anything near international standards. Brown was called in.

His style of coaching is described as frank and firm, and is credited with the formation of an actual team. With very limited resources, the Jamaican national team became serious contenders for the top Caribbean title, the Shell Cup. In 1991, they won it, beating arch-rivals, Trinidad and Tobago, which had come within one point of qualifying for the World Cup two years before.

The following two years saw the team making it to the finals, and in 1993 taking third place in the Gold Cup as well. That same year, unfortunately, he was forced to resign as head coach because of illness.

On Simoes' arrival as technical director, one year later, Brown made a re-appearance in his old position in the World Cup campaign. He has kept a low profile for the most part as Simoes took centre stage. There appeared to be no rivalry or tension between the two men, though, and they worked together to bring the team up to international level. Brown was content to remain in the background as Simoes was enveloped by media frenzy. When asked about the team's performance after games, however, Brown would be objective and analytical, stating frankly what their problems were and how he hoped to correct them.

The two who brought the Reggae Boys from amateur to professional footballer status, have strong Christian beliefs and refer to each other as "brothers in Christ". Some might say such a Brazilian and a Jamaican's coming together is a coincidence. Some say it's fate. Many believe it is faith.

Carl Brown trains as hard as his team

STEP ONE

The semi-final round, 1996

THE FIRST SIX GAMES

September 15, 1996, Kingston, Jamaica. The first of 16 games the Jamaican team had to play to qualify for the finals of the World Cup. They had already beaten both Suriname and Barbados decisively, both at home and away, with goals from Theodore Whitmore, Paul Davis and Walter Boyd. This was the semi-final round . . . they have never been past this stage.

Twenty-five thousand fans were packed into the National Stadium to witness the first match against Honduras. Most didn't really believe Jamaica have a chance at getting to France.

Left to Right: *Walter Boyd, Ian Goodison, Onandi Lowe, Fabian Davis, Gregory Messam, Peter Cargill, Steve Malcolm, Theodore Whitmore, Linval Dixon, Dean Sewell, and Warren Barrett*

28   The Reggae Boys

The beauty and the Barrett . . . Captain Warren Barrett meets one of Jamaica's beauty queens

Walter Boyd picked up a pass from wing-back, Gregory Messam, beat his marker and passed to Onandi Lowe. A powerful left leg set in motion rocketed the ball towards the Honduran goal, singeing the crossbar as it whizzed over—a goal missed by mere centimetres.

The cheers subsided, but a murmur hummed through "The Office". The Boys weren't playing bad at all! They just might be able to beat the Central Americans.

There was hardly time for doubts to return as Boyd collected a pass just outside the 18-yard box, turned and drilled the ball into the back of Honduran net.

The screams were deafening.

The Hondurans looked a little perturbed. The Boys' lead gave them confidence and they took control of the game. Two minutes to half-time and Theodore Whitmore held on to a short pass from a hardworking Lowe. Two defenders were closing in. Whitmore beat them and slotted home a second goal, right past the Honduran goalkeeper. The fans couldn't believe it! They were on their feet, shouting and cheering wildly.

In the second half, Lowe left his marker behind and passed to Boyd. "Blacka Pearl" calmly turned and placed the ball at the back of the net again. Jah! What could this mean?! Three-nil against Honduras, World Cup finalists in 1982?

The final whistle went and the Latin Americans hung their heads as they walked dolefully back to the dressing room. The jubilant fans filed out of the stadium, hoarse from cheering, but itching to spread the word of what they had seen.

It was just the first match, true; but a tiny seed of hope had been planted.

The Semi-Final Round

Tactical change . . . Simoes gives instructions to substitute Altimont Butler before sending him onto the field

St Vincent's goal under pressure

One week later on a water-logged Arnos Vale field in St Vincent, Jamaica's defence was under pressure and goalkeeper Warren Barrett looked anxious. Twenty minutes passed and the Vincentian fans were working themselves into a frenzy, when the Jamaicans got a corner. Walter Boyd took it. The ball came in, Paul Young went up, and a glancing header hit the back of the net.

The crowd was silenced. This was what had hit the Hondurans, they realised.

One minute to go before half-time, and Young picked up a loose ball outside the 18-yard box, left a defender behind and lobbed the ball over the Vincentian keeper to score his second goal.

In the 80th minute, the hosts got a penalty. They didn't let the opportunity slide past the uprights, but right between them. For the next 15 minutes the Vincentians tried to find an equaliser but they were denied. The Reggae Boys were determined to keep their lead and the three points from the match.

In Mexico City the following month, the undisputed veterans bombarded the young Jamaican players who just managed to fire back some shots. The Mexican generals, Zague, Hermosillo and Benal, led the foray; and goalkeeper Warren Barrett, who could not have dreamed as a child that one day he would be facing them, was trapped between the uprights of a suddenly huge goalpost.

Equal chance . . . Theodore Whitmore moves in for a 50-50 ball in the game against St Vincent at the National Stadium in Kingston ▶

30   The Reggae Boys

The Semi-Final Round

But incredibly, perhaps this is how his dream would have gone, he was making the saves—when they didn't volley wide. The defence felt his determination, and drew strength from it. Onandi Lowe, Hector Wright, Peter Cargill and Walter Boyd blocked out the sounds of Mexican fans screaming for their blood, and focused on holding off the attack. They came again! A green shirt tore threw and wham! The Reggae Boys' hearts sank. Goooooallllll!!!!

Fires flared again in the stands as T-shirts, flags and newspapers burned, and the chants rose to a crescendo as demi-god Zague gloried in the adoration of his people. But they had forgotten the other Latin American. The bespectacled Brazilian with the big moustache understood what was happening. Simoes made a substitution – he brought on Wolde Harris to partner Walter Boyd as striker and Onandi Lowe was moved to the sweeper position, replacing an injured Durrent Brown. It didn't work. In the 56th minute another attack hit home and the stadium roared: "Mejico! Mejico!" They didn't notice that Harris had passed to Boyd. *Por dios*! they sent Boys to do the work of men! Boyd was past his marker . . . The cheers were still ringing. Boyd picked his spot. Jorge Campos was waiting for him, they smiled wickedly. The ball rocketed past Campos. One hundred and ten thousand voices were silenced.

Goalkeeper and captain Warren Barrett helps out in attack

32   The Reggae Boys

The Reggae Boys' faces were grim. There was still one goal left to go. Lowe, at centre half, spread passes up front, slowing down the maddening tempo. The Mexicans were enraged: who did this man think he was? We are your equals, the Jamaicans answered, and they pushed for the equaliser. It never came; but the message from the Reggae Boys was clear when the final whistle blew, we will meet again. But next time, on our turf.

In another Central American country a week later, a sea of 25,000 Hondurans was blinding in blue and white, as they worked themselves into a Latin frenzy, led by folk dancers, cheerleaders and two mega-sized sound systems blaring folk songs and salsa. The Reggae Boys appeared unfazed. They had seen this before: flashback to the Azteca. But what the hell were these things hurtling towards them? They couldn't believe it! Plastic bottles filled with water! Soiled toilet paper! From every section of the bleachers, it was raining missiles. It was unbelievable! The Jamaicans, however, appeared unintimidated.

Half an hour into the game and Alex Pineda ploughed through the defence. He had Barrett at his mercy. Barrett advanced. Pineda beat him and let fly at a gaping goal. Jamaican hearts, already in a tizzy, skipped a beat. The ball was cleared miraculously off the line by a desperate defence.

Not enough. The ricocohet fell at the feet of Honduran midfielder Christian Santamaria on the edge of the 18-yard box. He took the shot . . . and kicked over the bar—to the sound of a thousand expletives from the bleachers.

The tide had turned on the Hondurans. Under pressure to score from their volatile fans, they pressed the attack. Brown, manning the fort of Jamaica's defence, bid his men stand firm. They managed to hold out untill the half-time whistle. The scoresheet was untouched but the Honduran fans were disappointed. They wanted to crush the little men from that little island down south.

The battle began again. The Boys were heading for a loss, it seemed. In the 70th minute, the final death knell rang for the Reggae Boys. Boyd, not hearing the referee's whistle, kicked the ball into the stands. He had already earned one yellow card; he got another. The rest of the team was in shock: They were dead for sure.

The rest of the game, a mere 20 minutes, stretched into hours, as the clock ticked too slowly for a Jamaican team under siege. Held captive in their own half, it was painful watching them hold off one relentless attack after another. Their spirits were flagging, the Hondurans were closing in for the kill . . . the whistle blew.

It was over. Nothing for the Hondurans. *Nada*. The Jamaicans almost wept with relief. They had gone into the enemy camp and denied them victory. They were going home with a point they needed.

After that it seemed only fair that they should get to beat up on somebody. The Vincentians were in Kingston this time, and a goalfest was on the cards. Theodore Whitmore took on the job of scoring with two beautiful goals in the first 16 minutes – the first a sweetly struck left-footer; the second a powerful half-volley that almost decapitated the hapless Vincentian goalkeeper.

Boyd, constantly in the limelight in the semi-final round

Paul Young added his name to the scoreboard. Then Peter Cargill. And who else? Steve Malcolm. Even the Jamaican fans were feeling sorry for the visitors. "Ease them up nah, boys." But the Reggae Boys were learning to go for the jugular, and they did.

The victory put them in second place to Mexico with 10 points and one game to go. All they need was a draw with the Mexicans to be one of the chosen six in the home-and-away final playoffs for a place in the top 32 destined for France.

It was not going to be easy. The Central American champions made it clear when they came to Kingston the following week. They used their trademark speed to run rings around the Jamaican defence. Their midfielders gave Warren Barrett minor heart attacks every time they closed in on his 18-yard box.

Yes!!! Ian Goodison climbs high to score the historic goal which ensured a 1-0 victory over Mexico and passage into the final play-offs for the World Cup

In the 16th minute, Barrett saw a cross coming in from the right. He misjudged it—Oh no! It was goal-bound. But no! Goodison cleared it off the line! What a rescue effort! An audible sigh went up in the stadium.

Corner after corner was blasted at Barrett. But Boyd was back. He combined with Steve Malcolm and Onandi Lowe to send the Mexican keeper diving. The fans were seeing hope now. The tension was incredibly high, men perched on the edge of their seats, sweat beading their brows.

Boyd tried again. Missed. Lowe bore down on a Boyd cross in the box—but was robbed by the keeper! The Central Americans decided enough was enough. They put pressure on the Jamaicans, taking shots from outside the 18-yard box. But none headed for home. With twenty minutes left, the visitors changed tactics and took a defensive stance, playing around with the ball and stalling for time.

Simoes made a move to substitute a limping Goodison. But just before the defender came off, he made history. In the 82nd minute he found the strength to leap heroically and head home a winner.

Thousands of fans were on their feet, cheering wildly. They knew, that was it! The Reggae Boys were home free. They were into the final play-offs, and they beat the Mexicans!

Disbelief mingled with incredible joy. Reggae Boys, they shook their heads ruefully, you've come a long way, babies.

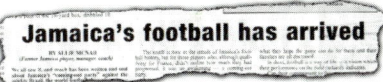

Only one story occupied the front and back pages of the Jamaica Observer *after the Mexico game*

From football rags to riches

The dreams the Reggae Boys had of making it to the World Cup weren't just about fame and glory; they were about food and clothes. The chance to play in France means being recruited by an English Premier League scout, or playing in Europe. Then they'd never have to worry about money again; as they did as children.

Like most Jamaicans, the Boys felt the bite of poverty as children. Goalkeeper and captain, Warren Barrett, can tell you about his father working in an asbestos factory, and his mother being a helper. Barrett got his first boots at 15 when he was picked to play for a national schoolboys team against Honduras. Before that he played barefoot; borrowing a pair of boots from a friend for important games. Entering the National Stadium through the front gates in the Reggae Boys bus still feels strange. The only way he used to be able to see matches was by climbing the floodlight towers and dropping in over the 30-foot wall. Now, he has contracts with Red Stripe and Puma sportswear.

Gregory Messam is one of six children who used to live with their parents in a two-room shack. They would go for days without food. His parents encouraged him to play football, but never thought he would make money out of it. He went straight from school into a local team with the hope of becoming a full-time pro'. He was lucky enough that a scout saw him and he moved to Florida. Messam's hero is, unsurprisingly, Pele, one of the world's greatest footballers who played as a poor child in the back streets of Brazil. Perhaps this is why the coming of Brazilian coach Rene Simoes was destined, for the Jamaicans have much in common with the Brazilians when it comes to poverty and football. As children, some of the Boys used to play football barefoot on dirt pitches in the ghetto; the ball an empty juice box stuffed with paper, battered into shape; the goal a pile of stones.

Up to three years ago, even after the World Cup campaign started, most had to hold down other jobs to survive. Bartenders, fishermen, factory workers, they had to work hard and play football for their country. One year later, they progressed to having boots and a real football but they were still playing for JA$2,100 (US$60) a game—a pittance one could barely live on for a week in a country whose economy has been deteriorating for the last decade.

With the arrival of Simoes came real salaries—Ja$120,000 a month (US$3500)—for top players. He made it clear to the JFF: it's players who pack the stadium—treat them well.

But even as their bills are being paid and they don't have to worry about where their children's school fees will come from, the players are still among the most lowly-paid in the World Cup. They still make less in a year than the stars they will face in France who make US$40,000 (JA$1.5 million) a week.

While Romario and Klinsmann are probably in a luxury hotel or health spa, 20 Reggae Boys are packed into a five-bedroom house not far from one of the most dangerous parts of Kingston, Grants Pen.

In a white bungalow with big steel gates and barred windows on which shirts and shorts are hung out to dry, the team spends more time here than with their families. Seven sleep in the living room with an old TV and a radio. After training at the National Stadium, they return here, to queue up for showers. Then, in a most incongruous fashion, while they eat and lounge around in towels outside, they might flip open personal mobile phones and spend a few hours chatting with their girlfriends or wives.

The cellular phone is a status symbol in Jamaica—to have one means you have the money to pay the hefty bills. So is a 'kris' car. Many of the Boys still can't afford one; and those who do, use it as a measure of their success. They park their cars in order of prestige on the lawn and in the driveway: the better the car, the closer it is to the house.

Another indicator of wealth is jewellery. Most of the Boys wear thick gold chains and rings and expensive watches. Messam has rings on his fingers, diamonds in his ears, chains on his wrists, and a heavy gold necklace on which he has suspended his cellphone.

It is a way of letting people know they have succeeded; that the hard times many people still face, are over for them. Prime Minister P. J. Patterson has publicly promised a two-acre building plot and low-cost home mortgages to each of the players; and a Reggae Boys version of *Cool Runnings*, the movie about the Jamaican bobsled team which is now a regular at the Winter Olympics, is pretty much wrapped up if they make a good run in the Cup.

While they still have dreams to fulfill, the Reggae Boys have put the nightmare of poverty behind them. The really hard times are over. At least for now

STEP TWO

The final round, 1997

Jamaica – 0   USA – 0
March 2, 1997, Kingston, Jamaica

Another year of tension-filled football matches is ahead, the first of which is against the USA. This is the real thing now—only three teams will go through after ten matches.

It's 96 degrees in the shade at the National Stadium and the Americans are wilting before 35,000 pairs of watchful eyes. But they make the first move, pumping long balls at Jamaica's goal. The hosts respond with patient ball control; Boyd, Andy Williams, Whitmore, Cargill and Dean Sewell opting for more possession and a wait-and-see approach.

The Americans work out a strategy, directing passes to the corners while their strikers cross to the centre. At the opposite end a duel is on between Boyd and defender Alexi Lalas, both men testing their skills against each other.

In the 38th minute, opportunity knocks and Whitmore answers. But not loudly enough. He finds himself in the 18-yard box, with a foot to the ball. As he moves to shoot, a US defender tugs at him, and the ball loses enough velocity to give another defender time to swoop down and clear it off the line.

Lowe comes on for Malcolm and is promptly taken down just outside the box. Boyd takes the free kick, and watches another chance cannon over the crossbar.

The troops are called in. More men are commissioned into the Jamaican attack. Cargill and Whitmore spread passes around up front. They win three corners but can't capitalise.

The US gets its golden chance in the 67th minute, as sweeper Durrent Brown finds himself racing at break-neck speed with an American striker. He forces himself into a full-stretch to deny the forward a scoring chance, hurting his hamstring in the process. Striker Young is brought on as a substitute, with Lowe taking over the defence.

Williams decides to make his move now, ploughing through the US defence. But the decisive goal never comes, and the match ends in stalemate.

Portia Simpson and Edward Seaga give the team a little morale boost

Man in the middle . . . Andy Williams moves through two American defenders ▶

Jamaica–0   USA–0

◀ *Another corner kick against the USA – Lowe in position beside Alexi Lalas*

Sewell races for the ball ▶

Durrent Brown

Position: Defender
Number: 21
Date of birth: July 8, 1964
Height: 5ft 7in
International debut: 1987 (vs Canada)
Club: Wadadah
Favourite footballers: George Weah, Theodore Whitmore, Warren Barrett, Linval Dixon
Hobbies: Playing cards, backgammon

The national team's sweeper gave the nation a scare when he was involved in a car accident along with teammates Warren Barrett, Steve Malcolm and Theodore Whitmore in February 1998. Football fans held their breath while he was kept in the hospital for tests on his eyes and head. Fortunately, he recovered and was soon back on the team. Sweeper for the national team since 1993, "Tatty" is a solid defender who played wingback for several years before taking over the sweeper position.

Durrent Brown harasses John Barnes in a 1993 benefit match

Jamaica–0 USA–0

Andy Williams powers past an American defender

Beautiful game, beautiful Reggae Boys fans ▶

Jamaica–0   USA–0   43

MEXICO

Mexico – 6   Jamaica – 0
April 13, 1997, Mexico City, Mexico

Mexico again. For the third time in six months. At the Azteca again. No team should be put through this twice.

In the last month the Jamaicans have taken on Bolivia, barely living to tell the tale of La Paz, thousands of feet above sea level. The air was so thin they had to take a rest after every run. They were humiliated by a 6-0 beating-in the first 20 minutes.

Toluca again. They prepared for the previous Azteca game there. Back to camp.

Toros Neza, never again. They decide to take on the local division one team in a practice game and end up on television and wires across the world after the match is stopped because of a massive brawl. Players, officials and even Simoes were injured in the fight. FIFA fines both Jamaica and Mexico, and the Mexican football federation Toros Neza.

It is a terrible blow for the Reggae Boys; and whatever hostile sentiments the Mexicans had before they arrived have multiplied, fuelled by the local media.

The question would be asked after the Mexico match, Who scored the first goal against Jamaica? Toros Neza.

Ten minutes into the World Cup qualifier and it is clear that the Reggae Boys are totally demoralised. A long cross from Luis Hernandez finds Carlos Hermosillo who is brought down by keeper Barrett.

The Brazilian referee points to the dreaded penalty spot. Goal number one.

The second comes in the 17th when it's clear Gregory Messam can't keep up with Hernandez; the third in the 30th as Hermosillo, the highest scorer in Mexican football history waltzes through an open midfield and stakes his second goal; the fourth he registers with a dive; the fifth when a substitute decides this is his best chance of going down in the books; and the sixth when Hernandez feels like finishing off the Reggae Boys.

In between the third and fourth Jamaica suffers another humiliation as Lowe, playing on the forward line, ignores Simoes' instruction to move to defence. He is immediately substituted.

The rest of the team can only watch numbly, their spirits already defeated.

The colourful face of Jamaica became warpaint in this game

Mexico – 6   Jamaica – 0

Oh no you don't . . . top defender Ian Goodison slide-tackles Mexican forward Carlos Hermosillo

Gregory Messam

Position: Defender
Number: 14
Date of birth: July 24, 1973
Height: 5ft 9in
International debut: 1995 (vs Cuba at Jarrett Park in Shell Cup)
Club: Harbour View FC; Dallas Burns, Colorado Foxes (USA)
Favourite footballers: Silas (Brazil), Hugh Blair
Hobbies: Watching and participating in track and field events, reading and listening to music

"Flamboyant" has been used to describe this defender with the dribbling skills who works the left wing. "The Energiser" says his is a tactical job he enjoys tremendously. His most memorable moment in the World Cup campaign was when Ian Goodison scored the goal against Mexico in the National Stadium. "It was a joyous moment for all of us, an historical moment for all of Jamaica. We were into the final round (of the playoffs)."

Messam doing his stuff

Theodore Whitmore tries to get 'a-head' of two Mexicans ▶

Mexico – 6   Jamaica – 0

The Bad Boys of Jamaican football

They started the campaign as star strikers, partners on the front line; but were sent off the field one after the other in a flurry of controversy. Just how popular Onandi Lowe and Walter Boyd were on the squad is unclear; but the fans loved them, particularly Boyd.

In April as the Reggae Boys began the campaign in the final round Lowe was suspended for four years after he allegedly walked off the field in the fiasco of a football match against Mexico where jump-kicks and fists flew between both teams. Lowe would not confirm that he did walk off the field; but did admit he was bitterly disappointed by biased reports of the match and the decision taken by the JFF. "First I was a hero, but now I am a villain."

Nevertheless, he would later apologise to the coaching staff and his teammates, and make a passionate plea for forgiveness, promising to play any position the coach told him to. His fans stood behind him; 100 placard-waving residents of Rockfort blocked the Windward Road, tried to block the bus taking the Reggae Boys to the airport but they were held off by the police.

After serving just six months of the ban, he was reinstated in early November. Halfway through the Gold Cup in February 1998, Simoes would state that Lowe could be the sweeper for the World Cup if he wanted, so impressed with his performance was the Brazilian coach. "He is tall, he is an excellent timer of the ball, he is calm, he has an excellent pass and when there is a dead ball, he can go out there and score goals. It is a dream to have a player like that. He is a leader."

Boyd too would find himself apologising to Simoes. At one time Jamaica's most expensive player (he was taking home up to five times the salary many of his fellow teammates were), he was suspended during the World Cup qualifying round in 1994 for an extended period of time for indiscipline.

But his troubles in 1997 came from a different source. Lack of form was the verdict. Blacka Pearl had not scored a single goal in seven months. He was dropped

Playing against Wales in a March 98 pre-cup friendly, the UK commentators kept referring to Onandi Lowe as 'a big lad' with a sense of affectionate awe in their voices, and actually lamented his unfortunate sending off in that game. Opposite, he forces his way past a Vincentian defender, and in the inset stops a Mexican dead in his tracks, proving the commentators wise beyond their words ▶

Mexico – 6 Jamaica – 0

from the team after the Englishmen were called in June. One coach claimed Boyd was "terribly unfit" and would not train.

His fans would not let him leave quietly. They clamoured for his recall; and by August 1997 he was back for a friendly against Colombia at the National Stadium. He then went to England for trials with West Bromwich Albion and scored five of 10 goals in their reserve team's thrashing of an Under-21 team. West Brom's coach was quoted as saying he was impressed with the striker with the striking red boots who "was exceptionally quick and had a terrific shot". It wasn't enough though; and Boyd left Britain without a contract.

He would also make another blunder by stating he was unhappy with the way he was being handled by Simoes who wanted to "play God" in his life. He was immediately dropped from the team again. On returning to Jamaica he made a public apology; but Simoes would not relent. The Brazilian believes, "When your child gets out of hand, sometimes he must be roughed up and pulled back in line".

Then, in October, just when Jamaican fans thought they would never see Blacka Pearl play again, he was recalled for a friendly against Haiti. But that too was shrouded in controversy. Another player was told one afternoon to give Boyd a message, that he was to come to training the following day. Boyd did not turn up because of what he considered the ad hoc, "unprofessional" manner in which he was recalled.

He would be sidelined for the rest of the year, despite the public outcry. But Walter Boyd is the proverbial prodigal son, and Jamaican fans refuse to forsake him. Inevitably, he returned to the fold. On January 1, 1998 he was recalled for a three-week training stint in Brazil.

He lasted two months. In early March he was axed for what seemed the final time when he didn't show up for the Carreras Foundation Awards. Boyd claims he didn't know his attendance was compulsory; Simoes says he did. The saga continued for a week as the public and the media blasted Simoes and the JFF for what they perceived as a feud with their "gifted son". But the technical director stood his ground and in a column in a local newspaper delivered his final say on the matter: "I am not here to please A or B. I am a worker who has to do his job with honesty and I am going to do that whether people like it or not."

One bad boy made it, the other didn't.

Walter 'Blacka Pearl' Boyd, always in the thick of it, renowned as a consummate ball player, seen here exhibiting his speed and control

Mexico – 6 Jamaica – 0

CANADA

Canada – 0   Jamaica – 0
April 27, 1997, Vancouver, Canada

Have the Reggae Boys recovered from the Mexican mauling? That's what is on the minds of fans at home and abroad. The Canadians are good candidates too for a rebound; they have failed to score in their last three games and have no points.

Neither side is impressive on the field; but the home team manages to fire off two shots at goal which go wide.

As the game progresses the tempo quickens and Boyd is moving into the spotlight. A powerful drive at goal is parried by the Canadian keeper who concedes a corner.

The Boys' confidence is returning, slowly but surely. Boyd, Williams, Malcolm and Whitmore are finally getting a rhythm going and passes flow.

Behind them is substitute goalkeeper, Aaron Lawrence, standing in for Barrett. He is called upon repeatedly to save the team from defeat, getting a hold on shots by forwards Alex Banbury and Gareth Kusch, and keeping them.

Altimont Butler, replacing Whitmore in the second half, stops hearts in front of television sets across Kingston. He picks up a pass from wingback Dean Sewell, dribbles and kicks goalwards. Alas! A defender prevents it from going over the line.

Canada, on home ground, fights desperately to win, firing shots from every angle. But Lawrence denies them all, and pulls the Reggae Boys through to take a much-appreciated point on enemy turf.

Defender Durrent Brown goes full out to block Alex Banbury's shot

Canada – 0 Jamaica – 0

Aaron Lawrence

Position: Goalkeeper (reserve)
Number: 13
Date of birth: 11 August, 1970
Height: 6ft 2in
International debut: 1990 (vs Zambia at Jarrett Park)
Club: Reno FC
Favourite footballers: Romario, Mark Wilson
Hobbies: Going to the beach, the garage

Competent, confident, Lawrence is capable of brilliant saves when necessary. When called upon to perform, he does not disappoint, as seen in the second half against Brazilian superstar omario's team, Flamengo, in January 1998 when the team went to Brazil for a training camp. "Wild Boy" made some smart saves which kept the score down to 3-0 against the masters of the sport.

Bumpy Head Gal salutes Reggae Boys

One sweet Jamaican vibe jus a wash over di land
Everybody mecking noise
We jus a pat wi back and beat wi chest
Fe wi Reggae Boyz

My Reggae Boyz dem train an get wicked pan di football
Cause dem nah teck no chance
Just a reggae dem way to the World Cup
On di road to France

Dem play wid style, technique an class
Like football suppose to play
A meck it clear say di green black and gold
Flag deh yah fi stay

So now we just a hold up wi han an big up wi chest
We license fi meck noise
Every one a we a pat wi back and beat wi chest
Fi wi Reggae Boyz

For a no cornflakes an bagels di Reggae Boys eat
But some good Jamaican food
Steam fish an crackers, okro, cow head soup an yam
A dat meck dem play so good

An when yu see di reggae foot go so "whoodoof!"
An kick di ball eena di net
Eh eh, "Probably dem never heard a we"
Dem siddung deh a fret

So now we just a hold up we head and big up wi chest
We license fi meck noise
We just a pat wi back and beat we chest
Fi wi Reggae Boyz

An when di Reggae Boyz play an win a match
Wedda at home or abroad
Every Jamaican no matter which part a world dem deh
Glad say dem come from yard

Jamaica unify, an di mount a green black an gold tings
Weh a sell pon every street
Tee shirt, arm band, towel, flag and belt
An green black an gold gold teet

Everybody figet bout politics and warmongering
Every enemy tun fren an stop cuss
We pan a football high because de Reggae Boyz
Mek a one bite a reggae dust

So we just a hold up wi han and big up wi chest
We license fi meck noise
We just a pat wi back an beat we chest
Fi wi Reggae Boyz

An if yu look pan how di word Jamaican spell
Check it, J-A-M-A- "I CAN"
An di Jamaican Reggae Boyz dem wild up football
For dem a big big Reggae Man

So we just a hold up wi han and big up wi chest
We license fi meck noise
Wi just a pat wi back and beat wi chest
Fi wi Reggae Boyz

◀ *Jamaican poet, comedian and broadcaster, Joan Andrea Hutchinson, aka Bumpy Head Gal after the 'chinee-bump' hairstyle she once adopted, also made her own tribute to the team*

Linval Dixon moves in on Canadian forward Gareth Kusch ▶

Canada – 0 Jamaica – 0

What's in a name? The Reggae Boyz

No one knows for sure where the name came from; and the JFF doesn't really care – they own it now. In March 1998 the JFF registered the Reggae Boyz as a trademark in 11 countries including Jamaica, the United Kingdom, Germany, France, Canada, the United States, Brazil, Belgium and the Netherlands, giving it the legal right to seize all items carrying the name illegally.

The prospect of any other group trying to use it seems unlikely. The name fits its owners so well that most people don't realise that it wasn't a Jamaican who gave it to them. Well, not directly, at least. The official story is that the Zambians baptised the Jamaican national team in 1995 when they were on a tour of Africa.

A local sports journalist is believed to have picked up on it first, probably via a wire story, and began using it to refer to the team. Then every newspaper started referring to them as the Reggae Boys/Boyz. Wire service reports followed the trend and now, it's the official nickname for the beloved underdogs of the World Cup '98.

In the same vein, no one is really sure who coined the term, 'the Office', for the Boys' home ground, the National Stadium in Kingston, but it certainly struck a chord with the fans who came to enjoy the Boys at work in their office.

The JFF hopes to make some serious money from Reggae Boyz endorsements

The Office

Canada – 0   Jamaica – 0

COSTA RICA

Costa Rica – 3   Jamaica – 1
May 11, 1997, San Jose, Costa Rica

The roller-coaster never stops. Just when the Reggae Boys are on a roll, they hit a pothole. Cargill and Whitmore are combining with Boyd and Williams to keep apace with the speedy Costa Ricans who are under pressure to redeem themselves after losing to El Salvador just a week before. Gradually, it is clear that they have studied the Mexicans' winning moves against the Reggae Boys and are using the same tactics—pumping the ball down the wings and slotting it into the six-yard box behind defenders. But it doesn't work. Strikers Hernan Medford and Paulo Wanchope are held off by a hard-tackling Jamaican defence.

Boyd is left to take a rocket of a free kick, forcing a good save from the Costa Rican keeper. Then Williams hesitates inside the box and is robbed of the ball. The coaster dips and the Boys' spirits spiral as Medford charges down the left, crosses; Barrett gropes, clears a path for Wanchope who knocks the ball into an empty net.

The Central Americans smell blood and move in for the kill, forcing the Jamaicans to make frantic clearances. Hopes soar for the Jamaican team as Whitmore finds himself alone with the Costa Rican keeper, but he kicks wide, and they plummet. Malcolm receives a cross from Cargill, hesitates at point-blank range and the ball is lost.

Simoes, looking for fresh legs (and hope), substitutes Young and Hector Wright for Butler and a flagging Boyd.

Barrett has not yet recovered and almost helps the opponents when he fails to hold on to a cross which rolls from his fingers and shaves the upright, earning the Costa Ricans a corner.

Cargill is not perturbed, and works to send Whitmore and Williams deep into the other team's half. The raiders finally strike gold at the 60-minute mark when Young passes to an unmarked Williams on the edge of the area. Williams beats a man and kicks delicately, the equaliser sliding in smoothly.

The roller-coaster has to come down. Complacence overtakes confidence and the Boys are caught knocking around the ball aimlessly. Wanchope rifles a shot past Barrett into the roof of the net from a seemingly impossible angle.

The general is not well. An ailing Cargill is replaced by Christopher Dawes. Without their inspirational stalwart, the Jamaican defence enters its final slide; and a Costa Rican substitute knocks in their third goal in the final minute to pull the brakes on any hopes of equalising.

Deejay Papa San's Reggae Boys Yah Yah, a tribute from a dedicated fan

---

A same so we play when we under we steam
You never know Jam Down have the wickedis team
We ball pass dem goalie (G O A L) like a gilotine
Uhnu see what I mean

Chorus

See Jamaica Yah ya
 Nuff boy see style an a fallah (F A L L A H)
 Mine you get a pile from we ballah (B A L L A H)
 A reggae boys run di place
 Dem caan tie Walter shoe lace, see Jamaica yah yah
 Nuff boy see style and a fallah
 Mine you get a pile from di ballah
 You see what I mean
 Oh boy you team did a dream

Black, green and gold it a di colour a we flag
It represent di stamina and di quality whey we have
Dem waan test Jam Down but a man dem a mad
We move fast like a lion we no crawl like crab

Chorus

We have a team whey healty and fit
Whay know all the style and trade and tricks
Most of dem move so swift, as you quint you get a shift
We have world best coach
Whey know all the tactics
We have the best centre forward
And the best wing back
who know fe defend and launch an attack
We have the two link man dem fi link up everyting...
Fi engineer the game and keep the ball moving
The two man dem pan the wing fast like an engine
By the twinkling of an eye dem will bust the pigeon
Mek we hear it fi di goalie cause him firm like wall
Galang Jamaica you a don stan tall

Chorus

When we inna difficulty we no worry an fret
We have nuff confidence – say we must buss de net
When we catch it pon we ches and put it back pon the lef (G O A L)
We know one bound fi select
Nandi Lowe and Walter Boyd we mek
you say you prayers
Hector Wright and Messam
will put you under manners
Paul Young and Goodison will treat you like a fryers
Barrett and Davis will fry you like a flitters
Jamaica yah yah

Warren Barrett

Position: Goalkeeper **Number:** 1
Date of birth: 7 September, 1970 **Height:** 6ft 2½in
International debut: 1990 (vs Barbados)
Favourite footballers: Bernard Lama (France's goalkeeper), Theodore Whitmore
Club: Violet Kickers
Hobbies: Reading, watching football, relaxing with family

The captain of the Reggae Boys has led them with confidence and a strong will through the grueling campaign to the World Cup in France. The keeper who frustrated Romario in the CONCACAF Gold Cup in January 98, repeatedly denied the Brazilian striker goal after sure goal, becoming the most popular player among the foreign-based media at the championship. Most were surprised that he has never represented another professional team outside of Jamaica.

The country's number one goalkeeper began his career at Cornwall College in 1986 where he spent three years, two of which were with the All-DaCosta squad. During that time he also played for the club Hornets then transferred to Violet Strikers in 1987, and the following year to the more well-known Violet Kickers. In 1991 he was given the position as goalkeeper for the national senior team; since then, no one else has challenged him for it.

Warren Barrett . . . a.k.a 'the rock' . . . will fry you like a flitter . . . although this game against Costa Rica was not one of his own personal favourites

Costa Rica – 3   Jamaica – 1

Linval Dixon shadows a Costa Rican

The Jamaican–Costa Rican connection

"Why oonoo neva come stay wid we dung a Limon? Nuff Jamaican dung dey. Oonoo neva haffi stay inna expensive hotel, man. If oonoo wid we, we woulda give oonoo good Jamaican food—yam, banana, dumplin and dem ting dey." That was Costa Rican journalist Claudio Grant's invitation to Earl Bailey when he went to the Central American country for their World Cup qualifying match against Jamaica.

Grant is one of the 50,000 third-generation Jamaicans living in Costa Rica, the largest concentration in the coastal province of Limon which they have made into a "likkle" Kingston. When Christopher Columbus landed in Costa Rica in 1502, it was the coastline of Limon that inspired him to name it the "Rich Coast".

Most of the black residents of Limon have English surnames and speak with a distinctly Jamaican accent. Their grandparents left Jamaica in the early 1900s to work on the banana plantations. Like many emigrants during that time who went to Central and South American countries to seek employment, they never returned.

In Costa Rica, the Jamaican immigrants would have discovered there were fundamental similarities between their culture and their adopted country. According to one of the many websites on Central America's second smallest nation, "Costa Ricans are not very punctual for social activities—except football matches, the cinema and weddings—but are more formal with their business appointments. "Mothers are regarded as the leading family figures; grandparents and elders are highly respected. The national pastimes are football and politics."

Today, the Jamaican community brings another cultural dimension to the Latin American country—food, language, and an innate skill and talent for sports. Star forwards on the Costa Rican team, Hernan Medford and Paulo Wanchope, are both third-generation Jamaicans.

Paulo Wanchope

Hernan Medford

Peter Cargill

Position: Midfielder
Number: 7
Date of birth: March 2, 1964
Height: 5ft 9in
International debut: 1984
Club: Harbour View FC
Favourite footballers: Rudd Gullit, Alan "Skill" Cole
Hobbies: Watching television, listening to music

One of the oldest and most experienced players on the team, "Jair" is indispensable not only because of his accurate passing and control of the midfield but his steely calm and composure in defence and attack. He works tirelessly, giving the other players the inspiration to fight.

The normally reserved Cargill is joy-stricken as he congratulates Paul Hall (22) at the Gold Cup in Los Angeles

Costa Rica – 3   Jamaica – 1

EL SALVADOR

Jamaica – 1   El Salvador – 0
May 18, 1997, Kingston, Jamaica

Support is at a low. The crowds barely fill one-third of the seats in the National Stadium. Only a win would be good enough to give the Reggae Boys a glimmer of hope of moving from their firm anchoring at the bottom of the playoffs.

The Salvadoreans, on the other hand, are confident they will do the necessary with these Boys. They have drawn 0-0 with Canada and beaten bitter rivals, Costa Rica.

But it turns out that they have seriouly underestimated the Jamaican team. It takes half an hour, but eventually the Boys find their feet, and take control of the game.

Before long, Williams, in a brilliant solo effort, picks up a loose ball near the half line, dribbles a few yards and then lets loose a grounder which veers right, out of the reach of the keeper, and into the back of the net.

The die-hard fans at the stadium feel a jolt in their chests. Half-time comes and Jamaica is still on top.

The second half brings promises of more goals as easy chances are created and squandered; but hearts leap into the throats of "Office" fans too, as several Salvadorean threats also loom against the Boys–but fortunately follow suit, evaporating harmlessly.

In the end, Williams' goal is all that matters, and Jamaicans are seeing a light on the horizon–Paris in the summer.

The unofficial Jamaican mascot, Tiger, rides into the Stadium on his donkey

Andy Williams

Position: Forward
Number: 9
Date of birth: September 23, 1977
Height: 5ft 8½ in
International debut: 1996 (vs All African XI at the National Stadium)
Club: Real Mona FC
Favourite footballers: Roberto Baggio, Paul Young, Walter Boyd
Hobbies: Listening to music, playing sports

Nicknamed "Bomber", Williams is considered one of the most exciting young stars of the Jamaican national team. The explosive dribbler signed with US Major League Soccer team, Columbus Crew, in February 1998 for two years. The former Rhode Island University student who left his mark on US college soccer is an attacking midfielder who takes his chances from as far as the edge of the 18-yard box.

The Bomber looking for a target

◀ *Williams demonstrates contact football Jamaican/Salvadorean style*

Jamaica – 1   El Salvador – 0

Malcolm leaves another Salvadorean behind

Steve Malcolm in the middle of a Salvadorean triangle

Jamaica – 1   El Salvador – 0

The Boys' bandwagon

In the months before they qualified, the Reggae Boys' stock value slowly went up. Companies from every industry in Jamaica gradually realised their selling value. American Airlines scored a major coup by beating the national airline, Air Jamaica, to official sponsorship (and had the Boys wearing vests with their logo plastered across the front and back); Grace Kennedy pledged to feed the team all the way to the World Cup; and the Adopt-A-Player programme saw every member receiving a decent salary just to play football, for the first time in their lives.

Green and yellow T-shirts sold in the hundreds of thousands; flags were manufactured by the truckload and stickers popped up on every bumper. After November 16, well . . . everybody and their subsidiary jumped on the bandwagon. Tickets to France became the most popular prize to be won in every advertising promotion. Corporate sponsors sprouted like mushrooms—the all-inclusive chains, Sandals and SuperClubs raced to present VIP cards to the players and technical staff; Desnoes and Geddes pumped JA$2million in one go into a "Making Noyz for the Reggae Boys" campaign—and the awards began to stack up on Simoes' and Burrell's living room walls.

Meanwhile, ads began to appear in international magazines promoting the Reggae Boys; and journalists from Japan, Croatia and Argentina—Jamaica's first-round opponents—arrived to do some background features on the Caribbean underdogs.

In the mad rush, the JFF battled to control the marketing mania. A secretariat was drawn from Jampro (Jamaica Promotions Corporation), the Jamaica Tourist Board, the Ministry of Labour, Social Security and Sports, the Tourism Division and the Ministry of Foreign Affairs and Foreign Trade to "handle the marketing and promotion of the Reggae Boys internationally."

The JFF attempted to halt the mass production of "bogus" team jerseys by having Kappa, the international sporting goods company, produce replicas of the new, official team uniform for fans to purchase. Plans were made to "take over" Paris by setting up a booth in Charles de Gaulle airport and a "sophisticated Faith's Pen" with ackee and saltfish, curry goat and rice and peas on a strip to be provided in one of the French cities where the team would be playing.

The travel trade, music and craft industries went into a tizzy. Millions of football fans from all over the world plan to converge on France for the finals. Most have never been to Jamaica; but if the business people have their way, by the time the World Cup is over, that would have changed.

An early development concept in the Red Stripe Making Noyz for the Boyz *campaign*

Corporate support multiplied after every success. The team's high visibility offered opportunities for the smallest and largest companies in the land. In the lead-up to the country's December 97 general elections even the political parties were anxious to associate themselves with the team — one wag even suggested that Simoes should run for the office of Prime Minister. Fortunately, he stuck to football.

Jamaica – 1   El Salvador – 0

CANADA

Jamaica – 1   Canada – 0
September 7, 1997, National Stadium, Kingston, Jamaica

The team has changed dramatically in the four months since the El Salvador game, with the inclusion of four foreign-based players. All were born in England to Jamaican parents which allows them to play for Jamaica under FIFA rules. Deon Burton, Paul Hall and Fitzroy Simpson are on the starting line-up while Robbie Earle is sitting on the substitutes' bench.

The four have been chosen from among several overseas players who were invited by the coaching staff for trials in June. They showed "plenty of quality and discipline," says Simoes. Ironically, most fans thought the most impressive of these was Burton who came not for trials but to get some physical conditioning.

His debut is about to be recorded in the hearts and minds of anyone who has ever cared about Jamaican football.

Jamaica takes the lead after half-hour of allowing the Canadians to chase the ball. A hard-running Simpson, a calm Cargill and schoolboy wingback, Ricardo Gardner, begin by taking control of the midfield. They break down the Canadian defence repeatedly, and only the Canadian goalkeeper stands between a Jamaican victory and a draw.

The Boys returned to the field with urgency in the second half. Burton and Hall are working hard and their skill is being unveiled. And then, the moment is upon us: Burton walks past a couple of back-pedaling defenders caught off-guard. Onside, Burton picks his spot and beats the keeper with a half volley.

There is nothing the Canadians can come up with to counter.

The Reggae Boys are back in the bus, ready to hit the road to France again.

A real Jamaican Reggae Girlz Reggae Boys fan

The team celebrates Burton's first World Cup goal for Jamaica ▶

Jamaica – 1 Canada – 0

◀ *Linval Dixon tries an aerial attack*

 ### Deon Burton

Position: Forward
Number: 18
Date of birth: October 25, 1976
Height: 5ft 9in
Debut for Jamaica: 1997 (vs Canada)
Club: Derby County

Picked to play for an all-star team when Europe took on the Rest of the World when the groups were drawn for the World Cup finals, Jamaica's "Ronaldo" lined up alongside his Brazilian namesake, Argentina's Batistuta and players from Japan, China and Cameroon against England's Paul Ince and Italy's Maldini.

At 16, the English-born lad of Jamaican parentage was snapped up by Portsmouth manager, Jim Smith, after Burton scored a hat-trick against his team. He went on to score 30 goals in one season for the youth team, 20 goals on the reserve side, 12 for the first team, finishing up the season before he landed in Jamaica with 10.

In five years, Burton was worth one million pounds, willingly paid by Derby County. Named Sportsman of the Year in 1997 by the Carreras Foundation (Jamaica), the powerfully-built striker turned down an invitation to join the Under-21 England team to play for the Reggae Boys.

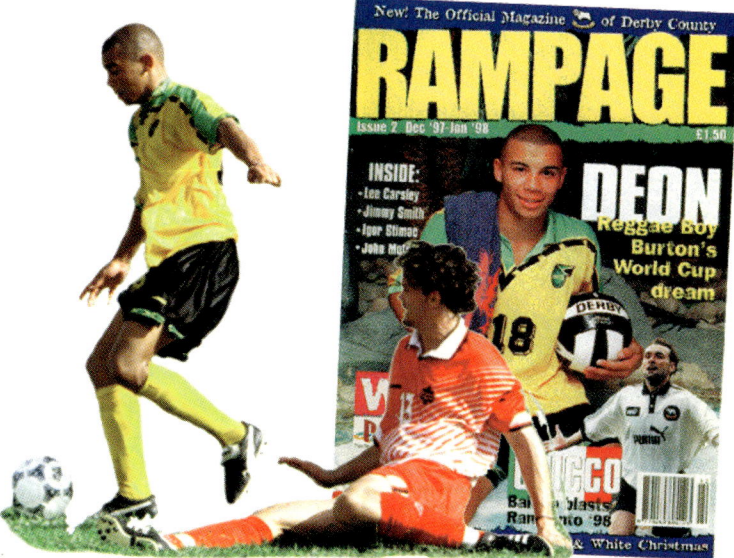

Jamaica – 1   Canada – 0

Enter the Boys from Foreign

Simoes had been dropping hints all along; but on March 11, 1998 in Paris, he made it clear: if he could get 10 overseas players to represent Jamaica in the World Cup, he would enlist them. Simoes had used the Reggae Boys' poor showing at the Brazil training camp two months before to point out that the team was not World Cup ready. "Now everybody in Jamaica know (sic) that the team need (sic) help and that will come from England."

The first wave was to bring 12 overseas-based players, many born or raised in Great Britain, their Jamaican parents making them eligible to play for the country. Nine showed up in early June 97 for training (only three or four spaces were available). In the National Stadium, before a sizeable crowd of hawk-eyed fans who came to see how the "Brits" compared to their local boys, Paul Hall, Fitzroy Simpson, Robbie Earle and a Deon Burton just looking for some fitness training, showed the fans what they had.

Fitzroy Simpson had made his league debut at 18. With more than 100 games under his belt, he began to attract the attention of larger clubs. He signed for Manchester City for a fee of 500,000 pounds in 1992, but was later bought by Pompey as part of a deal in 1995. Robbie Earle and Paul Hall were impressive too, but it was the young Ronaldo look-alike who caught the attention of the spectators—and Simoes.

Word got out that the English were here, and looking good. By the time the World Cup qualifying matches resumed in September, the 'UB-40' contingent, as they were dubbed, had changed—subtly—the image of the Reggae Boys. The local players realised the World Cup goal was for real. Here were at least a dozen English professional league players bidding for a place on the Jamaican team . . . that meant the Reggae Boys had a chance. And the fans realised it too.

Twenty-year-old Burton made his debut in fine style three months later. Backed by a more sophisticated midfield and defence, he did what he was brought in to do—score goals.

The second wave, in time for the Gold Cup, brought Frank Sinclair and Marcus Gayle who had been named for the Shell/Umbro Cup in 1996 but turned down the opportunity. Sinclair, a 27-year-old central defender and a Chelsea man for his entire career, had been playing since the age of 11. He made his League debut in 1991, was named Player of the Year in 1993, and picked up his first FA Cup winners' medal after a 2-0 win over Middlesborough in 1997.

Gayle, now 28, is an elegant forward with tremendous pace and skill, and one of the best flick-on headers of the ball in the game. A former England youth international, he made his debut for Wimbledon in winning style, helping them score a 1-0 victory against Leeds United in 1994.

Six overseas-based players, and there are still more coming. The dreadlocked forward from Ipswich, David Johnson (transferred from Bury for 1.4 million pounds), and Darryl Powell, a midfielder from Derby County, as well as Dean

Robbie Earle

Fitzroy Simpson

Sturridge, all have the Jamaican connection required to join the Reggae Boys. And they are interested.

Does it matter if the team is "truly" Jamaican? Some say the team is not the Reggae Boys anymore. But then again, UB-40 did reggae justice and took the music to an international level . . . even though they came from England.

Paul Hall

Local opinion was not always in favour of the boys from foreign

COSTA RICA

Jamaica – 1   Costa Rica – 0
September 14, 1997, Kingston, Jamaica

It's only been one week since they beat Canada, and confidence needs little boosting. The fans have returned to their supporting positions to rally the home team to revenge for their defeat in May.

The first 30 minutes pass as a scrappy, midfield scrimmage, with Cargill and Malcolm manfully trying to hold the fort since Simpson and Whitmore are finding it difficult to keep up with the pace.

The Costa Rican hone in on the weak links, putting Barrett to the test on several occasions. At the half-way mark Jamaica has managed only four full-hearted but half-paced shots; while their opponents have driven in nine shots, four forcing good saves from a beleaguered Barrett.

The Central Americans, having beaten the Reggae Boys before, push the Jamaicans deep into their own half, threatening to score at any moment.

In their quest for goal, the Costa Ricans leave their flanks open for a vigilant Burton to deliver a well-placed chip. Gooooaaaallllll!!!! Burton has done it again!

The Costa Ricans are reeling in shock. They can't believe it! They try desperately to conjure up an equaliser but Fate has joined the Reggae Boys' side and they walk away with three points, to the thunderous cheers of the Jamaican people.

Eleven points. Only three more needed from three games – two away and one at home.

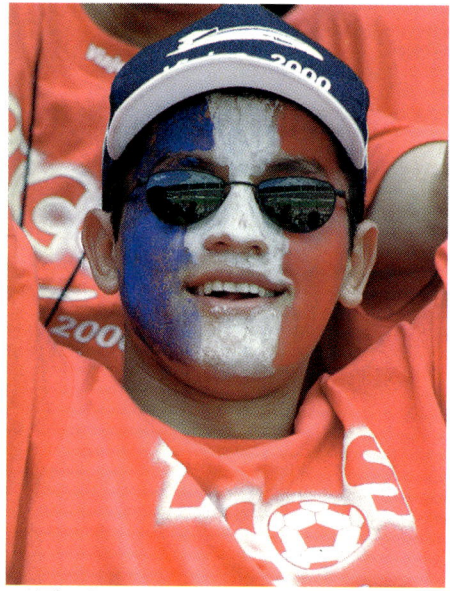

▲ *The Costa Rican supporters were proud to boast their own colours*

▼ *Mascot "Tiger" in all his glory*

Say no more

74   The Reggae Boys

Colourful Jamaican supporters in all their creativity

Jamaica – 1   Costa Rica – 0

*Robbie Earl under attack from
Costa Rican Mauricio Wright*

*Costa Rican goalkeeper
Erick Connis appeals
to the referee* ▶

76   The Reggae Boys

Theodore Whitmore

Position: Midfielder
Number: 11
Date of birth: August 5, 1972
Height: 6ft 2fiin
International debut: 1993 (vs Cayman Islands in the Caymans)
Club: Seba United
Favourite footballers: George Weah, Warren Barrett
Hobbies: Reading, listening to music

One of the regulars in the Reggae Boys line-up in the World Cup campaign, Whitmore is a skillful midfielder whose eyes are always on the uprights. "Tapper" was among the stars-in-the-making Simoes named for the Brazilian press in January.

Jamaica – 1   Costa Rica – 0

The die-hards among us

From the beginning, they were there. The die-hards. From as early as '96 when the Reggae Boys played their first World Cup qualifier against Suriname, they came. The Office wasn't packed though; the skeptics stayed away.

When Jamaica topped the semi-final round of their group, however, everything changed. Attendance rose to 30,000-plus per match. Sales of football T-shirts in the national colours doubled, tripled, and kept on going. Flag manufacturers couldn't produce enough. You could tell when a match was being played—that day everybody would be dressed in yellow and green, and flags would be flown on cars, buses, trucks and donkey carts. Hours before a match started the traffic would begin piling up around the stadium, with fans from the north coast having started out before dawn to get to Kingston.

Some came with drums and conch shells to keep a rhythm going; most just used their voices. A few painted their faces like the national flag. The dancehall posses wore leather and wigs, and posed outrageously for the foreign cameramen.

And always, the cheers. As kickoff time neared the decibel level would rise, confetti rained from the bleachers, and the black-gold-and-greens fluttered non-stop. At one match, we even witnessed a wave. Row by row, it rippled round the stadium, cheers rising to a crescendo as thousands of Jamaicans rose and fell together, as one.

It wasn't always like this though. There was a time when many thought the dream was over; and that "harsh reality" had hit—that this little island would never make it to the World Cup. One day early in the campaign the Reggae Boys looked up into the stands and saw that it was barely one-third filled. It was in the early stages of the play-offs between the final six Concacaf teams and they were floundering at the bottom of the table. Somehow the die-hards showed themselves. Things were bad but they still believed. And that must have meant something to the 11 men in yellow and green who walked onto the field to face El Salvador. Maybe those die-hards realised they had to scream a little louder and rally harder to get those going, and keep them there. Who knows? Jamaica won the match.

When you have the same dream twice, you wonder if it means anything. And many people were having it—once again. After every match the Reggae Boys played, they would see more in the dream as details became clearer, and it would leave a stronger impression. For once the news coming out of Jamaica would not be about murders and an economy in a tailspin. Out of the ghettos the Jamaican spirit was rising, just as it did in reggae and the bobsled team. The phenomenon called football fever that has raged in countries of Brazil and Italy for decades was taking hold of Jamaicans. Here was something true and strong, that brought a people together, stirring their faith and making them believe again in what Jamaicans could achieve—internationally.

The dream came true. Now, another is taking shape . . . can Jamaica win the World Cup? Ask a die-hard.

The sign says it all . . . Fans pack the bleachers

Jamaica – 1 Costa Rica – 0

Reggae Girls surround a stunned Ricardo "Bibi" Gardner at the end of the final game against Mexico

Potrait of a die-hard fan

Don Streete is definitely a die-hard. He has not only been to every Reggae Boys practice session and home match, but also to their first round away match against St Vincent (he and a dozen friends chartered a plane); to Mexico City where the Boys were beaten 6-0; to the Washington DC home-away-from-home game; and the Concacaf Gold Cup matches in Miami.

"Soccer is very close to my heart," he smiled, "always has been." His obsession with the game took him from kicking ball at Calabar High to a football scholarship to Howard University in the US. He still plays and coaches, while juggling his job at the National Water Commission (where the team sometimes practises), going to Reggae Boys matches and e-mailing excited expatriate Jamaicans who want to hear what's happening with the team.

"I always believed that Jamaica had an abundance of talent. When I heard about the new programme I realised that there was a group that could harness and mould that talent," he recalled. "I visualised we would have topped the Caribbean, that we were the best in the region. That's why we went to what many thought was an insignificant match like the one against St Vincent."

Streete's conviction (or intuition, you could say) led him to collect enough memorabilia from the World Cup campaign to fill a tote bag: T-shirts, souvenir footballs, ticket stubs, flyers, beads, caps, even a mini Mexican sombrero.

And he intends to add some more. Already he's booked his tickets for the first round of World Cup games in France, gotten his French visa, a road map to all the matches and is *pret à partir* (he studied French at college). He pointed to his copy of the schedule of World Cup matches (on which all Jamaica's matches are marked off, of course). "I'll be there if they make it to the second round."

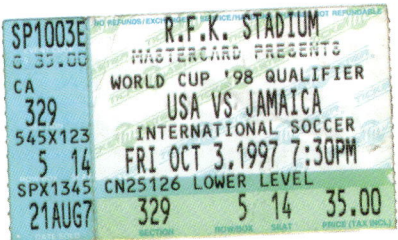

Don Streete

Don cheering with Jerry D, MC for most of the games played at 'the office'

Jamaica – 1   Costa Rica – 0

USA – 1 Jamaica – 1
October 3, 1997, Washington, DC, USA

The fans are coming in droves into the Robert F. Kennedy Stadium, from Boston, Brooklyn, and as far away as Kingston. In buses, on motorcycles with pillion riders waving Jamaican flags as they weave through the traffic to the RFK, in cars, by train, by plane–by Jah! they were coming.

Jamaicans from all across the United States of America, as well as other West Indians rallying behind the Reggae Boys, are here, wearing and/or flying the black, gold and green colours of Jamaica's flag.

Rastafarians join the melee, while smart vendors are peddling any and everything that resembles "yard".

Accents, long lost in adopted Yankee twang, are being unveiled again. "Who? We a go beat up them boy ya tonight, man. Jus' wait."

The American fans streaming in are visibly perturbed by large groups of flag-bearers who have taken it upon themselves to share their version of popular dancehall songs. Inside, it is clear that this is not a home game for the US team. There are as many Jamaican supporters as American, the stadium awash with yellow T-shirts.

The Reggae Boys look around the stadium, unable to believe their eyes. This was like a home game! And what is that sound echoing across the field? Dutch pot-covers?!

They turn and face the Americans confidently. The first half passes uneventfully. In the 49th minute, though, the referee makes an extremely dubious penalty call for the Americans. Eric Wynalda takes it, and scores.

One half of the stadium erupts in joy; the other is silent.

The very next minute Burton, who is by now known as "the one million pound man", capitalises on a poor backpass from a defender to goalkeeper, Kasey Keller. The cheers, screams and drumming are even louder than those of a minute before.

The Reggae Boys are not satisfied though. They are looking for a win; but it is denied.

The final whistle blows. Hundreds of police officers are outside, expecting some form of violence. But none is forthcoming from the thousands of Jamaicans walking proudly home.

82   The Reggae Boys

They came from far and near . . . US based supporters cheering the Boys in Washington DC

Jamaica – 1 Costa Rica – 0

The local Jamaican community in Washington DC set up nuff entertainment for the fans from Jamaica and USA

Deon Burton goes on the attack in Washington DC

Jamaica – 1 Costa Rica – 0

Ian Goodison

Position: Defender
Number: 5
Date of birth: November 21, 1972
Height: 6ft 3in
International debut: 1996 (vs Guatemala)
Club: Olympic Gardens FC
Favourite footballers: Juergen Klinseman, Walter Boyd
Hobbies: Playing football, riding a motorcycle and going to nightclubs

The same year he made his debut, this defender scored an unforgettable goal against Central American giants, Mexico (rated fourth in the world), which helped Jamaica to qualify for the final round of the Concacaf playoffs. "Pepe" possesses strength physically and character-wise. He has a keen eye for the game and is always ready to move from the defence into a scoring position.

Ian Goodison in flight

Ricardo Gardner

Position: Defender
Number: 24
Date of birth: September 25, 1978
Height: 5ft 9fiin
International debut: 1996 (vs Costa Rica)
Club: Harbour View FC
Favourite footballers: Diego Maradona, Ian Goodison
Hobbies: Listening to music, watching ice hockey

The youngest member of the squad (and perhaps the World Cup), Gardner is a prodigy of the game. A brilliant and accurate passer who reads the game well, "Bibi" is another of what Simoes calls his "stars-in-the-making" who plays with a very Brazilian philosophy—confident with the ball, calm and always looking for space.

Young Gardner sends two Costa Ricans sprawling

◀ *Ian Goodison is head and shoulders above his American counterparts*

Jamaica – 1   Costa Rica – 0

The wedding of reggae and football

It may have begun with Bob Marley and his well-known football fetish. Every DJ worth his salt knows how to kick ball, including Buju Banton. Every year DJs, singers and masters slug it out on a field, abandoning mikes and headphones to reveal what skills they have in their big toes.

Given the chance to marry both Jamaican loves, many entertainers turned up at the National Stadium and away matches to rally fans behind the Reggae Boys. From Beenie Man to Bounty Killer, Yellowman to Jimmy Cliff, they came out to support the national team. Many have done remixes of hits in tribute to the Reggae Boys including Red Rat, the Main Street Crew and Mighty Diamonds, which they performed at the stadium before matches and during half-time, much to the delight and ear-deafening appreciation of the crowds. They made the matches into concerts, creating a mass hype that intimidated faint-hearted opponents and lifted the spirits of the home boys.

"Ah my team dat," cried an excited Beenie Man, in a bright yellow and green track suit, slapping his chest to emphasise his pride. He was on his way to the dressing room at the stadium to congratulate the team on their much-needed victory against Costa Rica.

At a friendly international against Sweden, the legendary Jimmy Cliff (upon whom an honorary doctorate has recently been conferred by the University of the West Indies) could be seen standing next to the Jamaican bench on the track. He didn't stay standing for long as excitement got the better of him, and he was soon jumping, skipping and flexing, apparently warming up to go on the field. Simoes never did put him on though.

Having used one passion to rally the Jamaican people behind another, the icons will no doubt be in France to keep the fires alive. Maybe even singing in French.

They could be twins . . . Ian Goodison and ace DJ Bounti Killa

Bob Marley's love of football was legendary

Papa San serenades the Boys

Ian Goodison and top DJ Beenie Man

The Scare Dem Crew keeps the crowd revved up at a home game

Jamaica – 1   Costa Rica – 0

Will the real Reggae Boys please rise up?

As if the Reggae Boys weren't stealing enough of the spotlight as the "Cameroon" of World Cup '98 (i.e. most loved, and most unlikely to win), FIFA went and commissioned theme songs for every team. Lawd have mercy! Reggae superstars galore came out to put this song together. From the writers/producers—Sly Dunbar, Handel Tucker, Mikey Bennett—to the musicians—Dean Fraser, Ernie Ranglin, Monty Alexander, Peter Ashbourne, Jon Williams and Paulette Bellamy—this is reggae's version of "We Are The World". Artistes in the constellation called Jamaica United include Buju Banton, Shaggy, Maxi Priest, Diana King, Tony Rebel, Ini Kamoze, Ziggy Marley, The I-Threes, Richie Stephens, Brian Gold and "Toots" Hibbert. The uptempo number speaks of the indomitable spirit of the Jamaican people. Tucker says "Rise Up" was deliberately non-specific so that "after the World Cup the song will still motivate and uplift people". Written to inspire anyone who feels down and in need of encouragement, as Dunbar puts it, "Rise Up" was expected to take French and other airwaves by storm upon its release on the FIFA album under the Sony label in March 98. Reggae-jazz, hip hop and nyabinghi remixes were also to be released later that month in the Caribbean.

Rise Up!

Hopes are rising higher and higher, there is magic everywhere
The expectation of a nation is Music to the ear
We're singing a brand new song
Marching to a brand new beat
Down the hillside, through the valleys
Filling every single street
Rise up! Rise up!
Stand and take your place
Shine like the sun
Your journey has just begun
Rise up! Rise up!
Stand like the brave, Rule your destiny
Be the best that you can be
The world is yours for the taking
Giving up is the only crime
Write now on the pages of history
This is your moment, now is your time
Now we know that it is not an easy road
3 o'clock, another road block
You gotta carry de load
There's a winner inside you
Just waiting to answer the call
You've heard the voice, now make the choice
Follow that star, believe in who you are
Rise up! Rise up!

Jamaica – 1 Costa Rica – 0

EL SALVADOR

El Salvador – 2   Jamaica – 2
November 15, 1997, San Salvador, El Salvador

They need just one point-a draw. They will deal with Mexico when the time comes.

The first half lacks flair and effort. The Salvadoreans can take charge but they're holding back.

In the second half we see why. Two minutes go by and Brazilian-born Nildelson de Mello cuts a neat header past Barrett who just catches a glimpse as it goes flashing into the back of the net. One nil! Forty-two thousand fans are on their feet.

In less than four minutes, however, Fitzroy Simpson floats a free kick across the goal and Burton delivered his response—a brilliant header that sails over the goalkeeper.

The Salvadoreans sit down—hard. Victory has been snatched away. It remains elusive until the 78th minute when Hall picks up a ball near the half line, beats a lone defender and unleashes a scorcher that's too hot for the keeper to even touch.

Now the draw has evaporated.

Three minutes are left in the game. The Boys are already dreaming of Paris in the springtime when reality strikes with a bang! The ball hits the back of the Jamaican net.

It is going to be a race to wire. A win would have put the Reggae Boys on the plane to Paris; but a draw means everything depends on at least drawing with the Mexicans. A defeat for the Jamaicans, coupled with a US capitulation to El Salvador would see the latter easing Jamaica out of the coveted third CONCACAF slot.

The celebrations begin again. The Central Americans push for a third goal. His defenders in trouble, Barrett is forced to push a ball destined for goal over the bar.

The final whistle goes, and the Reggae Boys shake their heads ruefully. So close, so far away. They had it in the palm of their hands and let it slip away.

But they had reached this far; there was no turning back. Onward to Kingston —for Mexico.

Steve Malcolm breaks free of his marker

El Salvaor – 2 Jamaica – 2

Psychological Warfare

It must be something about Central Americans; in San Pedro Sula for a return game with Honduras, the entire Jamaican contingent was herded into an uncovered area and subjected to a narcotics search by sniffer dogs. The local media had branded the team as a group who "smoked ganja with abandon and had to smoke it to play well". On the eve of the match as the team practised under floodlights, without warning, the stadium was plunged into darkness. Disoriented and a little fearful, players and officials scrambled to recover their clothing and equipment in the dark.

For this crucial return game that could have decided the final CONCACAF place for France, El Salvador was even less subtle. Only 200 (of a few thousand) tickets for the game were made available to Jamaican fans. Captain Horace Burrell had to make a hasty trip to San Salvador to secure more, but the word had already been sent back to Kingston: you come at your own risk. The threat of being pelted with bags of urine and faeces and other missiles was real, and Jamaican fans, while wanting to rally round the team, pulled out of the charter—leaving their players to brave the Salvadoreans alone.

They did; and went on to play despite large crowds of local fans shouting and making noise outside their hotel to keep them awake the night before the match.

Paul Hall

Position: Forward
Number: 22
Date of birth: July 3, 1972
Height: 5ft 9in
Debut for Jamaica: 1997 (vs Canada)
Club: Portsmouth FC

In the short time since he has returned to the country of his parents' birth as part of Jamaica's World Cup campaign, this striker has made himself an indispensable part of the starting line-up and a favourite of the fans. "It has been a dream of mine to play for Jamaica ever since I was old enough to know that my parents came from Jamaica. It is a dream to even train with the team so my dream is partially fulfilled." When Hall first came for trials he had finished the season with his English club as second top scorer with 15 goals. In the few World Cup qualifiers in which he played, Hall left his mark.

The Reggae Girls

While it's true Jamaican women have stood behind their football men all the way, don't think that's all they've been doing. From the fans to the Minister of Sport, women have been key to the whole World Cup campaign. Starting from the top: Portia Simpson. She could be seen at all the matches, even in El Salvador when very few dared to brave bottle-throwing and toilet paper from the fans. On the track one could find the Reggae Girls, young, able-bodied beauties who danced and screamed themselves hoarse and posed for foreign photographers. Oh, and the Bashment Girls, in bright wigs and outrageous leather get-ups, letting the Boys know they were worth getting dressed up for.

In the stands, the loudest and most vocal cheering squads were women. Most agree they go to watch the Boys in their shorts and not the game. Most surprisingly though, are the women on the field. For years young Jamaican women have quietly received football scholarships to US colleges where the excell. In 1997, in the aftermath of qualification euphoria, the Jamaica Football Federation launched a national schoolgirls' football league. In a keenly watched March 98 final at the National Stadium, potential stars of women's football made themselves known, the level of their skills surprising many in the National Stadium that day, among them a few of the Reggae Boys.

The new face of Jamaican football?

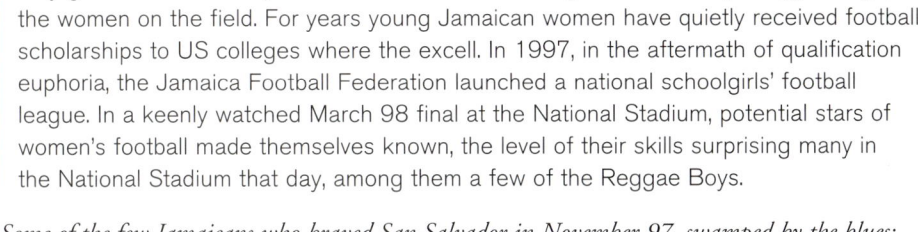

Some of the few Jamaicans who braved San Salvador in November 97, swamped by the blues: lower centre right in hat, Portia Simpson, Jamica's then Minister of Sport

El Salvaor – 2   Jamaica – 2

MEXICO

Jamaica – 0   Mexico – 0
November 16, 1997, Kingston, Jamaica

This is where it all ends. The National Stadium in Kingston.

Two other games are being played Canada is up against Costa Rica, and the Americans, who have already qualified, face a desperate El Salvador. The latter need a win, and for Jamaica to lose.

As Fate would have it, the two matches are being played almost simultaneously so that neither Jamaica nor El Salvador will have the benefit of knowing how the other has fared before they make their final bid for the third CONCACAF spot.

The entire Caribbean country is watching. Thirty-five thousand, all wearing yellow T-shirts, are packed into the National Stadium, waving flags and making one hell of a din. Flags have been flying on cars for the last week. This is not about the Reggae Boys any more; this is about the pride and hope of 2.3 million Jamaicans, and the millions of the diaspora.

It is clear that the Mexicans, assured of their place in France, are more interested in avoiding defeat than winning. They were reluctant to engage in the warfare which would undoubtedly have occurred if they attempted to storm the Jamaican defence. When captain Luis Garcia finally took a shot at goal in the 20th minute, it was with some reluctance and not much conviction.

Though there was nothing to cheer about on the field, the home fans were exulting in every goalless moment the Mexican let pass. France was clearly in their sights. The loudspeaker crackles, but is barely heard above the happy stadium noise. Then what a hullabaloo breaks out! The cheers build up across the stadium as word is passed. The announcer comes on again. Thousands of miles away in Boston, the US has scored its first goal against El Salvador!

The Eiffel Tower is on the horizon.

The Reggae Boys appear not to have heard, focused as they are on keeping the Mexicans away from their goalpost.

Then, a hush comes over the crowd. Rumours of an equaliser come next.

Minutes later, the screams are louder: USA has scored again.

The celebrations begin again. "France, we comin!"

By now, everyone has stopped watching the match and is prancing around to the joyous sounds of dancehall. For a moment, the thought that they might actually run on to the field before the final whistle blows and stop the match paralyses the paranoid. After all the Reggae Boys have gone through, to be disqualified would mean a curse by the gods.

This beautiful fan had much to smile about

The USA score a third goal; there is no hope for El Salvador.

People stop and stare at each other: Jamaica is going to the World Cup finals

Finally, the painful game on the field ends. The masses can't contain their joy. They flood the field, lifting the Reggae Boys on their shoulders. Players, officials can't believe what's happened. They hug each other, and tears flow freely as the DJ goes wild, blasting tribute after tribute to the team. The Reggae Girls are going crazy, bubbling and whining with sheer abandon. Whitmore picks up a flag and runs the entire length of the field, other Reggae Boys gleefully joining his victory run. Prime Minister PJ Patterson declares the following day a national holiday. Horns start to blow across Kingston and headlights flash on the streets as a salute to sons who had made their country very very proud.

Deon Burton holds off a Mexican

Every eye on the ball . . . Gardner goes down, but so does the Mexican: Simoes seems calm

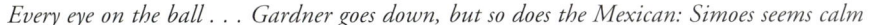

Jamaica – 2   Mexico – 2

Dancehall Queen Carlene (in cap) and friends, anticipating the result, start the celebratory gyrations

Sewell (12) and Hall face a Mexican duo

The Reggae Boys

Go, Reggae Boys, go!

The better the football, the more beautiful the fans

Jamaica – 2 Mexico – 2

102 The Reggae Boys

The dream comes true – Rene Simoes is held high by supporters after Jamaica drew with Mexico and qualified for the World Cup finals

Theodore Whitmore is carried like a king through the tumult of celebration

Jamaica – 2 Mexico – 2

Epilogue

"There are some blind teams in the Gold Cup like Honduras, Jamaica, Cuba . . ." the 1994 World Cup Most Valuable Player, Romario, dissed the Jamaicans on radio. He had also called them rough and crude. "When we heard that," says Warren Barrett, "he just got us upset right away and we definitely went out with fire in our eyes to prove a point not only to him but also to the other Brazilians and the rest of the world that **'Hey! We are here!'**"

The soccer world reeled from shock. In their first Gold Cup match in Miami, the Jamaican team held the great Brazil to a goalless draw. Minus Ronaldo, Leandro, Juniniho, and Ze Roberto but with Romario, Denilson, Edmundo and Zinho all in attack, the Reggae Boyz fended off attack after attack, Barrett denying Romario shot after shot.

Then after drawing with Guatemala, Brazil was accused of playing even worse than in the 0-0 draw with Jamaica. *Jornal de Sports* said, "Drawing with Jamaica was embarrassing. Another draw against a team which has never qualified for the World Cup is a humiliation for Brazilian football . . . what should we expect from a competition where Brazil is the exception? What's the point of playing Jamaica, Costa Rica . . . Brazil should have been warming up for France by playing top sides."

The Reggae Boyz must deal with the arrogance of traditionally strong football countries. The sport is a career for most of the players they will meet in France.

But they must remember beating Guatemala 3-2 and El Salvador 2-0 and losing to Mexico only in sudden death extra time. The world is watching and as Nigerian coach, Bora Milutinovic, said on his arrival in Jamaica for a friendly in February: "I would like to offer congratulations to the Jamaican team because of their progress. You had a 0-0 tie with Brazil. You have improved so much."

They must remember Sunday, January 31, 1971, when Santos FC, with the legendary football hero, Pele, was defeated by a local team, Cavalier FC. They must remember Paul Hall and Deon Burton forcing Taffarel to make saves. They must remember the words of one of their greatest footballers of all time, Alan "Skill" Cole Jr: "There are a lot of social problems in Jamaica, you hear our entertainers express it in songs. And like the music, football helps to alleviate some of the stress and problems our people face. That is why the passion for football is becoming as great as for music. Victory helps to wipe away the tears."

More than victory, the renewal of Jamaican patriotism has helped this country to believe in itself again. And that is all the Reggae Boyz have to do, believe in themselves. They made it to the World Cup finals, and they stood up to the greatest team in the world. They can do it again.

The Boys are making good use of all their pre-cup matches so that nobody will refer to them as a 'blind' team ever again